CONTENTS

Content Manchester City FC **Photos** Victoria Haydn, Tom Flathers, Matt McNulty (Manchester City). Getty Images, PA Pics
Produced by Reach Sport **Managing Director** Steve Hanrahan **Commercial Director** Will Beedles **Executive Art Editor** Rick Cooke **Executive Editor** Paul Dove **Editorial Production** Simon Monk **Editorial Design** Adam Ward, James Maluchnik **Marketing & Communications Manager** Claire Brown **Printed by** PCP

"WE HAVE TO SAY CONGRATULATIONS TO LIVERPOOL AND THANK YOU SO MUCH, THEY PUSHED US TO INCREASE OUR STANDARDS. IT'S INCREDIBLE, 98 POINTS, TO GO BACK-TO-BACK. WE MADE THE STANDARD HIGHER LAST SEASON AND LIVERPOOL HELPED US. TO WIN THIS TITLE WE HAD TO WIN 14 LEAGUE GAMES IN A ROW. WE COULDN'T LOSE ONE POINT. IT'S THE TOUGHEST TITLE WE HAVE WON IN ALL MY CAREER, BY FAR. I AM SO PROUD OF THE PLAYERS AND THE FANS"

-PEP GUARDIOLA

12.08.18

ARSENAL 0

MAN CITY 2

(Sterling 14, Bernardo 64)

Attendance: 59,934

STERLING
7
KICK-OFF
TO THE SEASON

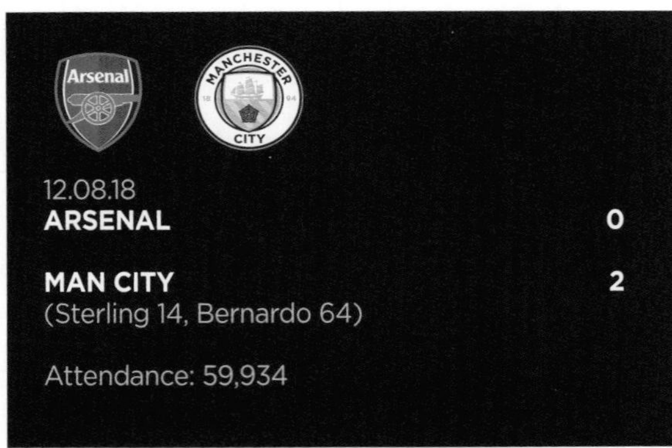

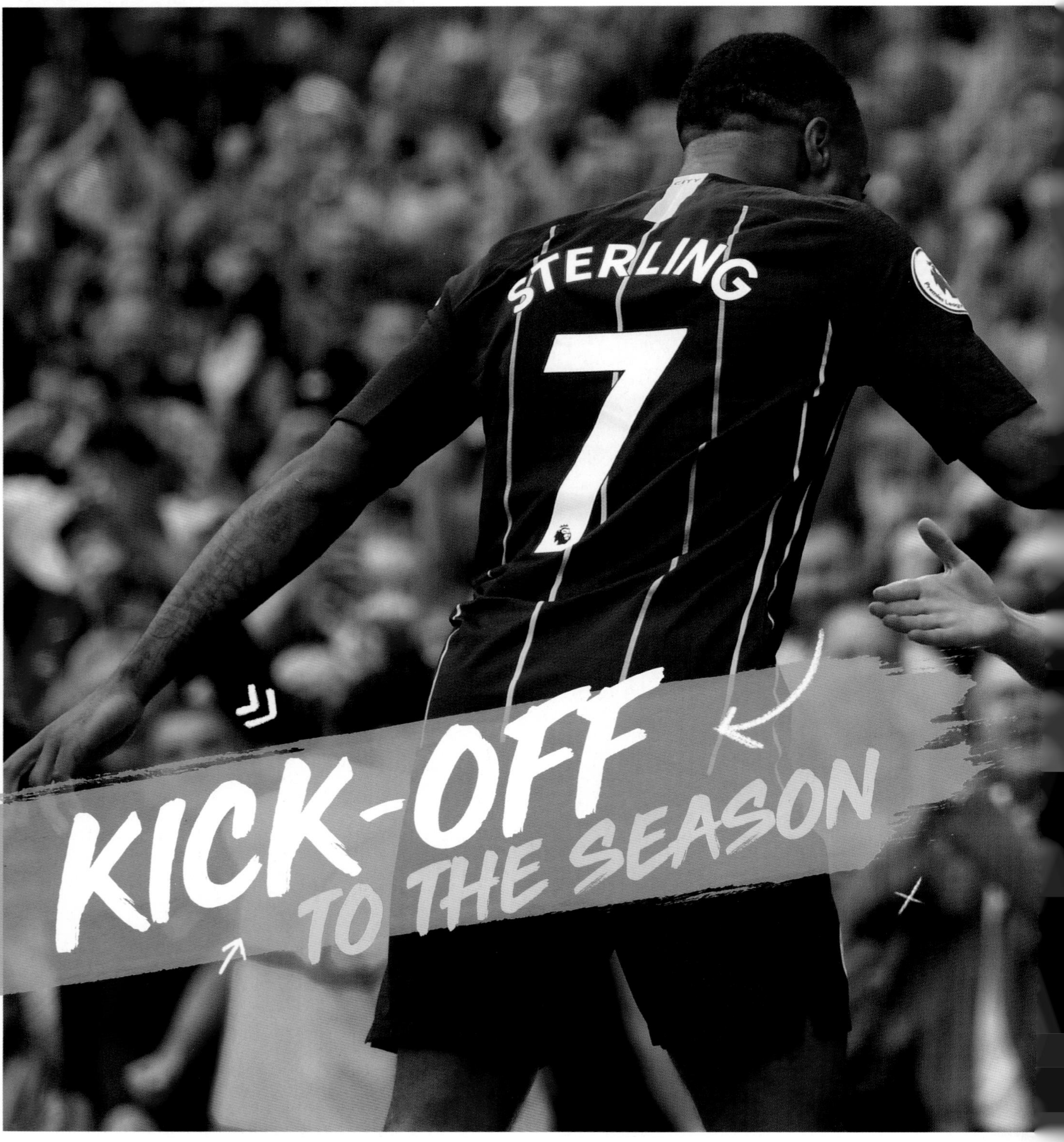

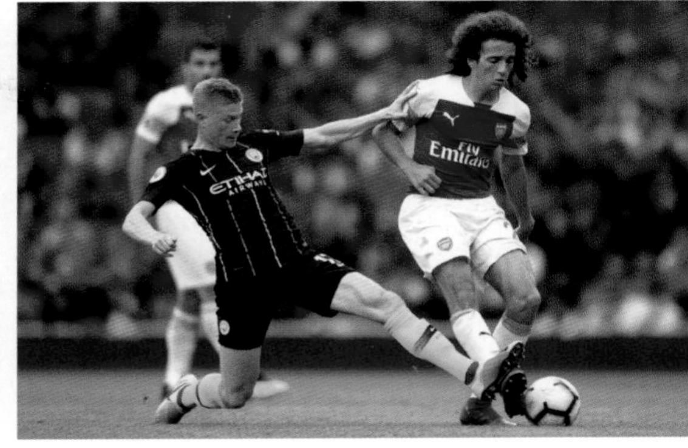

Many pundits had already written the 2018/19 title race off, believing City – who had won the 2017/18 title by 19 points – were simply too far ahead of the pack and even if Pep Guardiola's side didn't quite reach the heights of the previous season, who was going to stop the champions this time around?

Former PFA Player of the Year Riyad Mahrez was added to the squad during the summer, but was the only major signing for City who, quite rightly, felt there was no need to fix something that clearly wasn't broken. A little fine-tuning here and there but that was all that was needed.

The curtain-raiser to the English season, the FA Community Shield, pit City with a difficult-looking clash with Chelsea at Wembley, but a 2-0 win – courtesy of a Sergio Aguero brace – gave the Blues the perfect start to the new campaign.

A week later, City returned to the capital to take on Unai Emery's new-look Arsenal at the Emirates Stadium. The Gunners were under new management and represented a sizeable obstacle to begin the Premier League title defence at – but goals from Raheem Sterling and Bernardo Silva secured an impressive 2-0 win and sent out an early message for the rest of the Premier League that it was business as usual for the

19.08.18
MAN CITY 6
(Aguero 25, 35, 75, Gabriel Jesus 31, D Silva 48, Kongolo 84 og)
HUDDERSFIELD 1
(Stankovic 43)

Attendance: 54,021

Blues. Liverpool, however, started equally well with a comfortable 4-0 win over West Ham United at Anfield, giving Klopp's men equal cause for optimism – and pole position in the first published table of the campaign.

With City's home campaign beginning with a 6-1 win over Huddersfield Town a week later, the champions were already sending out ominous warnings that there would be no Centurions hangover – not on Pep's watch.

Liverpool responded with a 2-0 win at Crystal Palace, but they were one of six teams in total to take maximum points from their opening two games. Chelsea, Spurs, Bournemouth and Watford also boasted embryonic 100% records.

City ended the month with a trip to the Black Country to face newly promoted Wolves in a Saturday lunchtime kick-off. It's probably fair to say Wolves enjoyed being described as 'the Championship Man City' with their free-flowing,

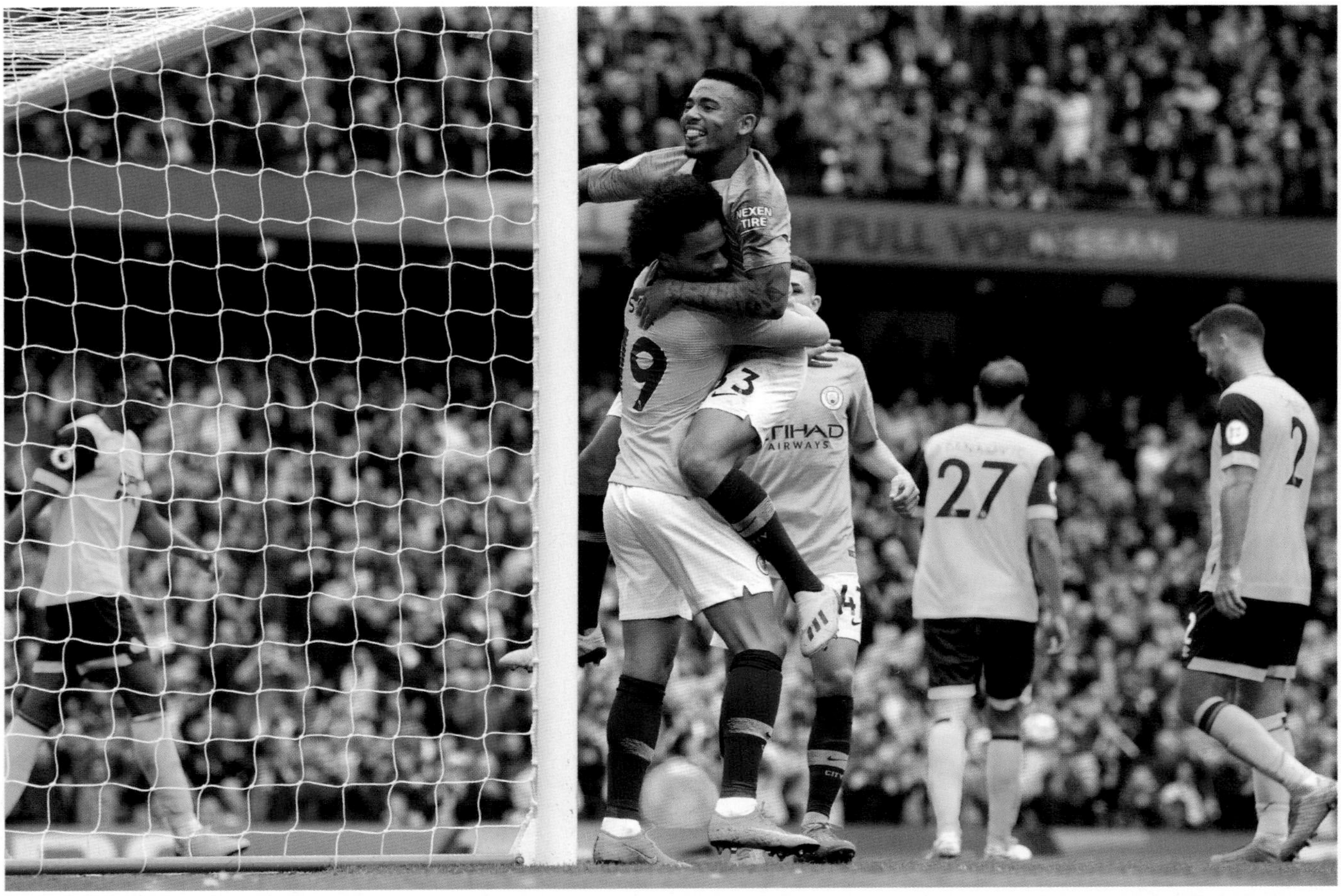

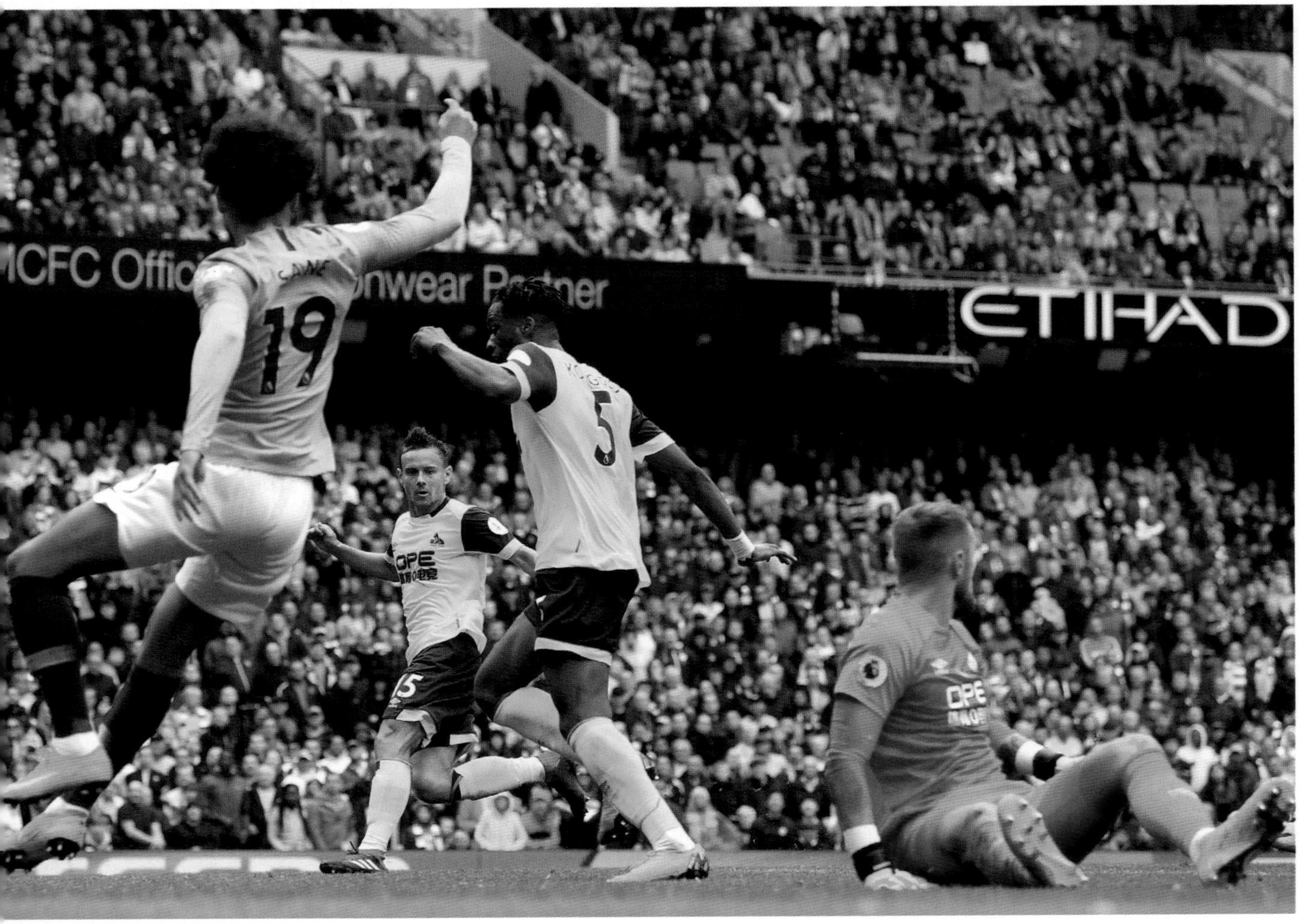
MCFC Offic
nwear Partner
ETIHAD

easy-on-the-eye style earning Nuno Esprito Santo's side a handful for anyone at Molineux.

The Blues had won their previous eight competitive games on the road, but were far from their regal best against a confident and neat Wolves side – and when Willy Boly's stumble inside the six-yard box appeared to end in the back of the City net via the defender's arm, Pep Guardiola could only lament the fact that VAR for Premier League games was still a year off – particularly when TV replays showed Boly had indeed handled the ball. No matter – the goal stood.

A loss to a newly promoted side three games in was not in the script – the champions were behind and needed a response. Incredibly, it had been eight months since the Blues had last trailed a Premier League game...

Fortunately, a thundering header from Aymeric Laporte on 69 minutes drew City level and though the game ended 1-1, Aguero hit the post David Silva might have had a penalty on another day in the time that remained and combined with the Boly goal that shouldn't have stood, the general feeling was the Blues had been slightly hard done by.

After the game, Pep said: "It was a very good point. We created chances but their keeper made saves, so today we draw. We knew how good they were last season. No complaints. We created a lot, that's why it's good. In the first half, Aguero hit the post – sometimes it goes in, sometimes not."

Liverpool, meanwhile, laboured to a 1-0 win over Brighton a few hours later. Three games in and Klopp's side had a two-point advantage. It didn't feel significant, but they had started marginally better.

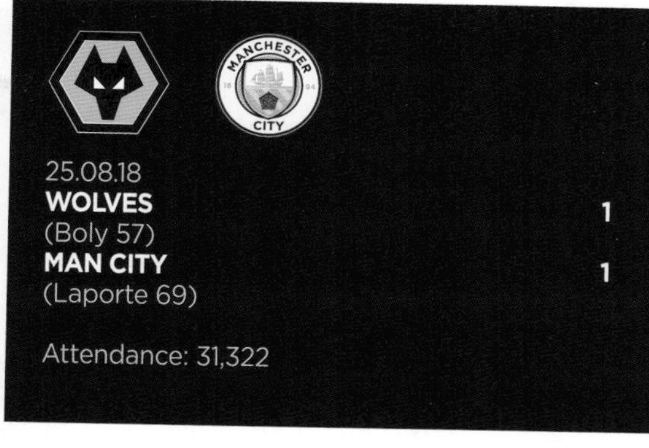

25.08.18

WOLVES 1
(Boly 57)

MAN CITY 1
(Laporte 69)

Attendance: 31,322

'IT WAS A VERY GOOD POINT. WE CREATED CHANCES BUT THEIR KEEPER MADE SAVES, SO TODAY WE DRAW. WE KNEW HOW GOOD THEY WERE LAST SEASON. NO COMPLAINTS. WE CREATED A LOT, THAT'S WHY IT'S GOOD'

THE RACE BEGINS...

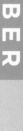

SEPTEMBER

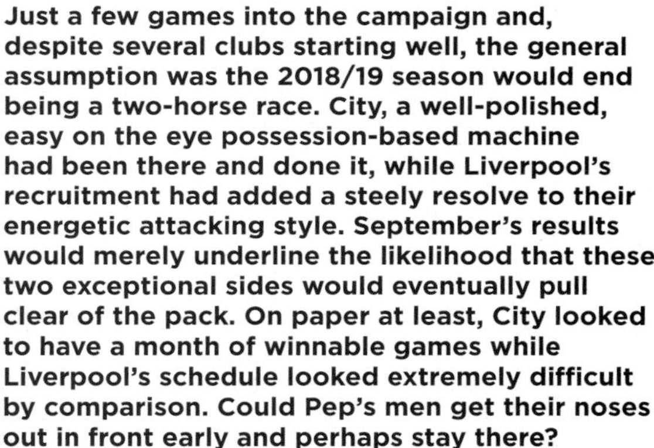

Just a few games into the campaign and, despite several clubs starting well, the general assumption was the 2018/19 season would end being a two-horse race. City, a well-polished, easy on the eye possession-based machine had been there and done it, while Liverpool's recruitment had added a steely resolve to their energetic attacking style. September's results would merely underline the likelihood that these two exceptional sides would eventually pull clear of the pack. On paper at least, City looked to have a month of winnable games while Liverpool's schedule looked extremely difficult by comparison. Could Pep's men get their noses out in front early and perhaps stay there?

Chelsea, Spurs and Watford were all there or thereabouts after impressive starts, but it was City who began the next round of fixtures with a hard-fought 2-1 win over Newcastle United at the Etihad. Liverpool also had to battle for a 2-1 win at Leicester, while Chelsea's 2-0 win over Bournemouth ensured that only they and Liverpool had maintained their 100% starts

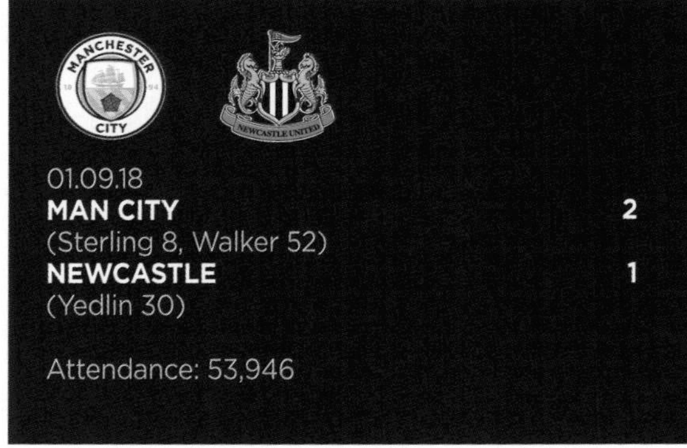

01.09.18

MAN CITY (Sterling 8, Walker 52)	**2**
NEWCASTLE (Yedlin 30)	**1**

Attendance: 53,946

»

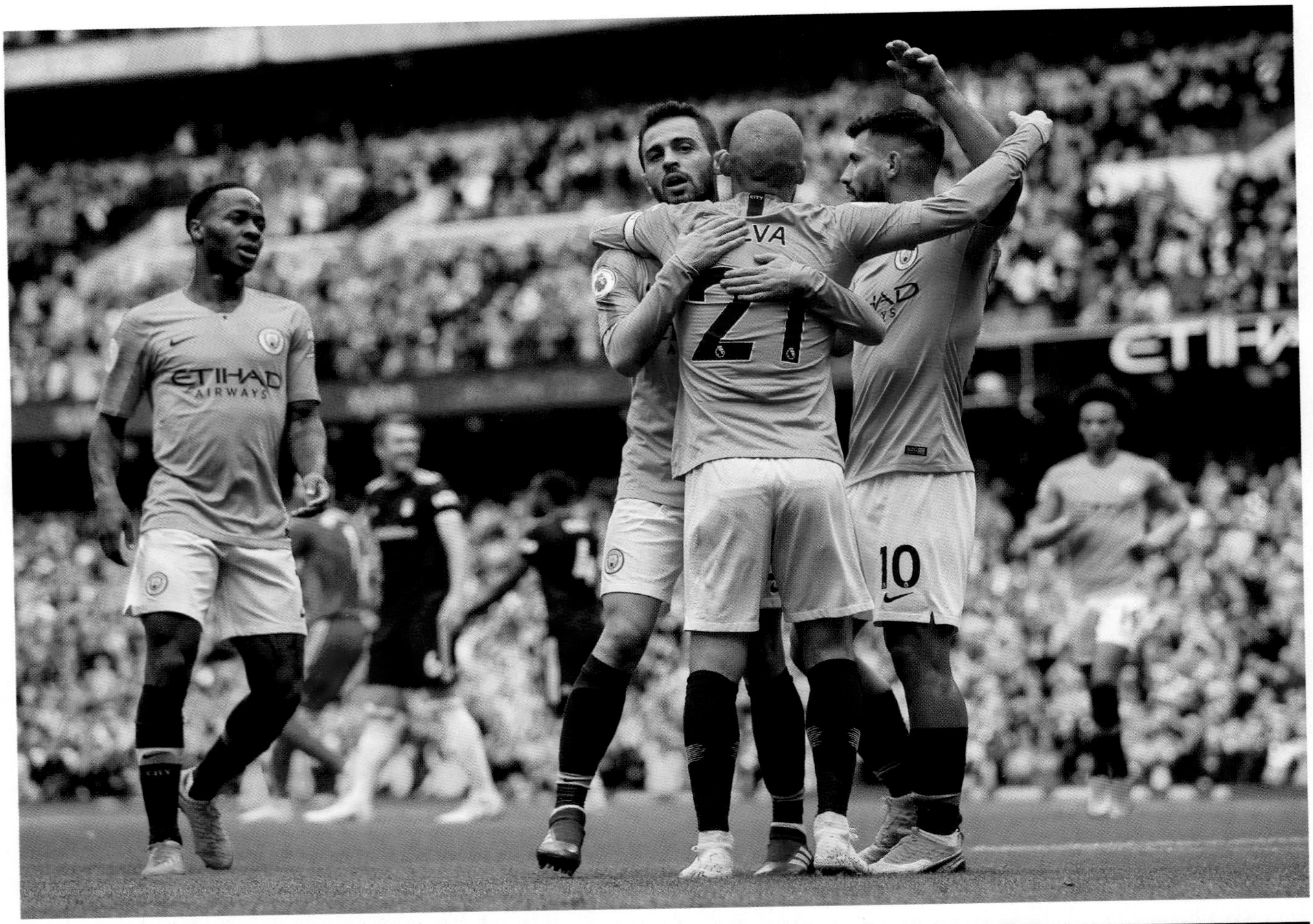
ETIHAD
AIRWAYS
VA
21
10
ETIHA

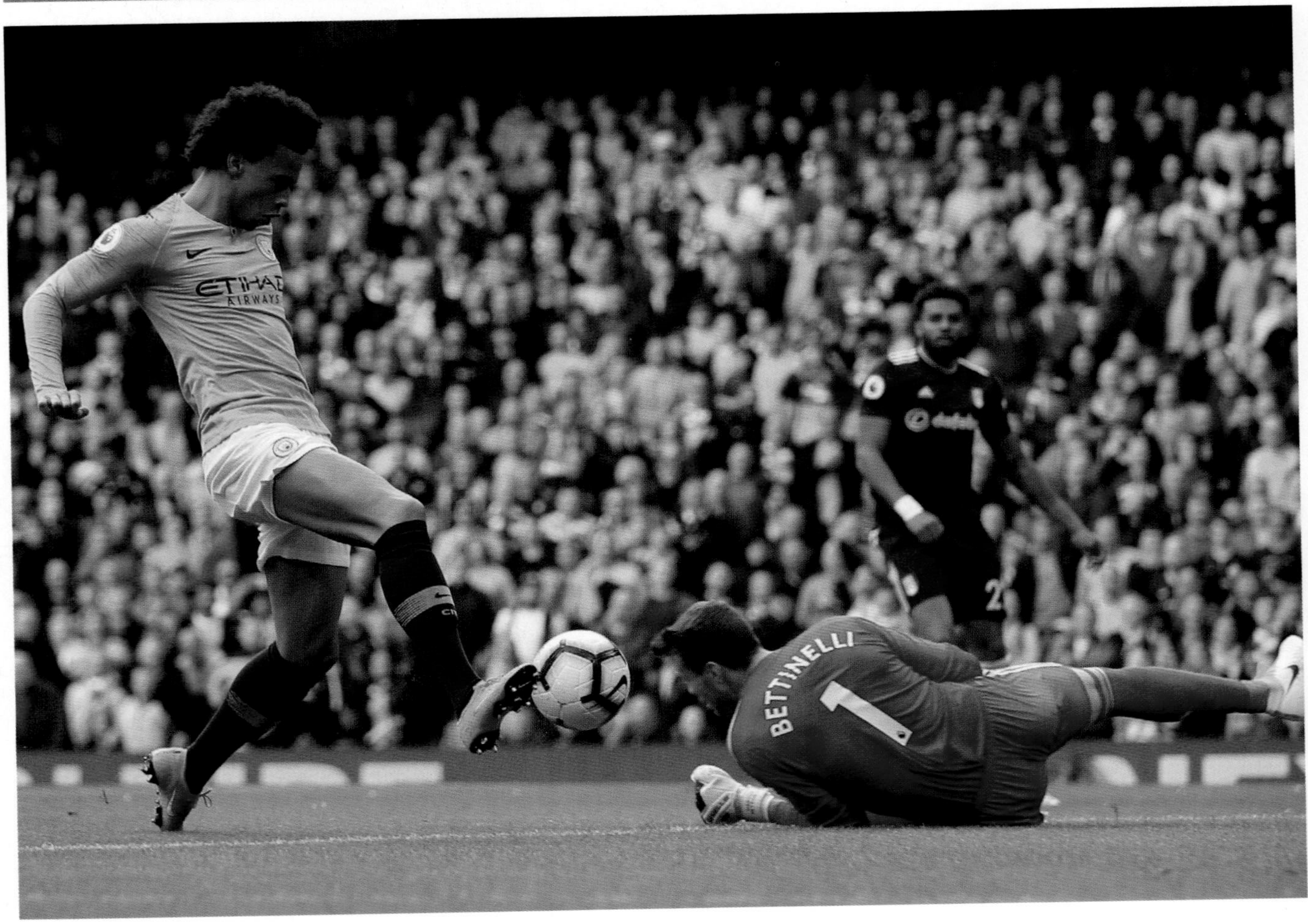
ETIHAD
AIRWAYS
BETTINELLI
1

leading into the first international break of the season.

The TV schedules would often have Liverpool and City starting at different times throughout the campaign and it was Liverpool who were first in action after the break with another impressive away win - this time at Tottenham - and though City brushed aside the challenge of Fulham (3-0), Chelsea's fine start continued with a 4-1 win over Cardiff City which left Maurizio Sarri's side top of the table on goal difference. Perhaps it would be a three-horse race...

The Blues had started their Champions League campaign with a loss to Lyon at the Etihad and desperately needed to bounce back quickly and a trip to South Wales to face Neil Warnock's struggling Cardiff City offered the perfect opportunity to get back on track just a few days later.

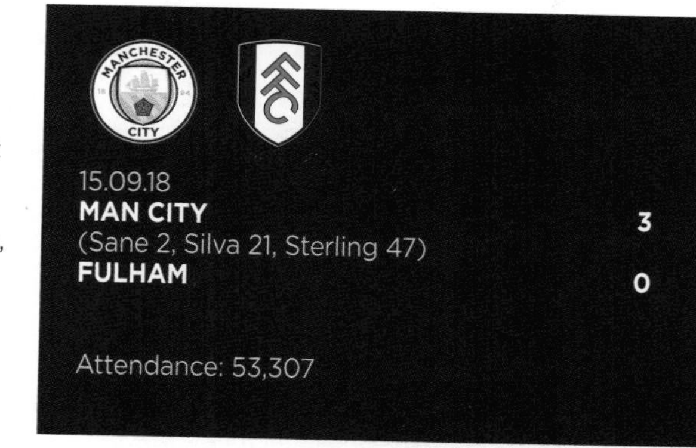

15.09.18
MAN CITY 3
(Sane 2, Silva 21, Sterling 47)
FULHAM 0
Attendance: 53,307

'WE WERE AGGRESSIVE WHEN WE HAD THE BALL AND WE CREATED CHANCES. TODAY WE HAD MANY, MANY CLEAR CHANCES TO SCORE AND WE NEED TO WORK AT SCORING MORE'

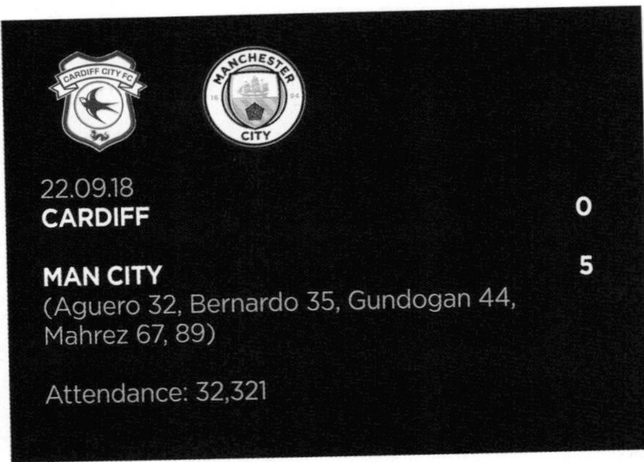

22.09.18
CARDIFF 0

MAN CITY 5
(Aguero 32, Bernardo 35, Gundogan 44, Mahrez 67, 89)

Attendance: 32,321

On September 22, a rarity as City and Liverpool kicked off at 3pm – and both enjoyed comfortable wins with the Blues thrashing Cardiff City 5-0 with a display that oozed confidence. Though the Bluebirds held out to the 32nd minute, City eased through the gears thereafter with Sergio Aguero, Bernardo and Ilkay Gundogan on target before the break. Riyad Mahrez added a couple more in the second-half to complete the rout. At Anfield, Liverpool cruised home 3-0 against Southampton and Chelsea's 0-0 draw with West Ham meant the Reds were now two points clear at the top.

City ended the month by beating a stubborn Brighton 2-0 with Aguero and Raheem Sterling on target against a side whose one intention was damage limitation. Liverpool, who kicked off a couple of hours later showed their resilience by grabbing a last-gasp equaliser away to Chelsea to earn a precious 1-1 draw and preserve their unbeaten start, however those dropped points meant that City moved top on goal difference, thought the biggest test of the campaign was quickly looming into view...

SEPTEMBER

'OUR POSITIONAL GAME WAS FANTASTIC AND WE DIDN'T CONCEDE MUCH IN SHOTS. BRIGHTON DEFENDED SO WELL AND I GIVE A LOT OF CREDIT TO THE WAY WE ATTACKED TODAY. WE ARE SO FAST ON THE COUNTER-ATTACK'

ETIHAD PLAYER OF THE MONTH
10
SERGIO AGUERO

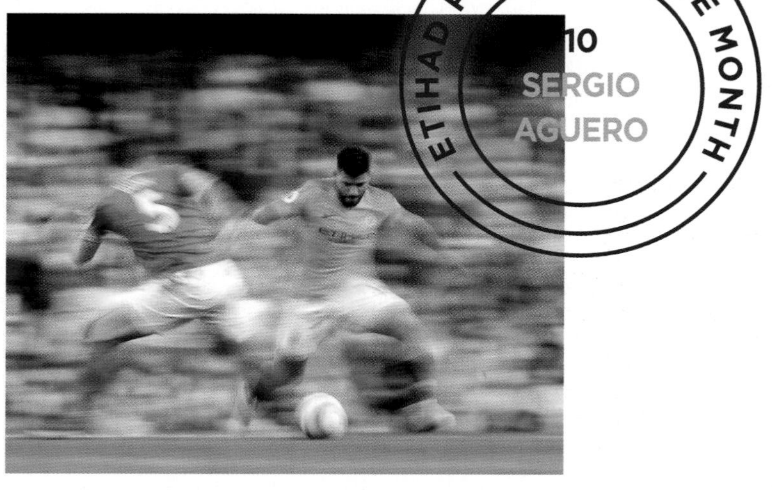

29.09.18

MAN CITY (Sterling 29, Aguero 65)	2
BRIGHTON	0

Attendance: 54,152

»

CLOSE ENCOUNTERS

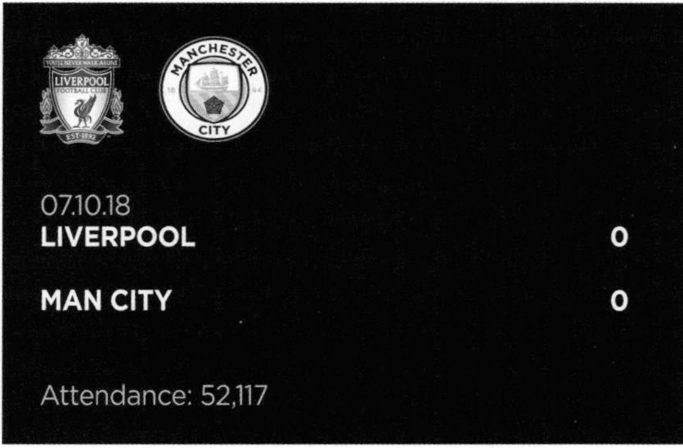

07.10.18
LIVERPOOL 0
MAN CITY 0
Attendance: 52,117

Liverpool had twice given City extremely tough encounters at Anfield earlier in the year, with the Blues conceding seven goals – a 4-3 loss in the Premier League and a crushing 3-0 Champions League defeat. If there had been a criticism from the two losses suffered, it was perhaps that City had been too adventurous and been punished as a result. How would Pep line his team up for this encounter?

It was still very early in the campaign when the Blues travelled to Anfield, but the occasion had a special feel to it, as though the meetings between City and Liverpool would shape each other's season – losing was not an option.

The respect each team had for each other was clear throughout, with neither side prepared to go all-out attack and test the other's resolve, but while the Reds escaped two decent penalty shouts from City, but when Leroy Sane was bundled over in the box by Virgil van Dijk with

just five minutes remaining, saw the referee point to the spot. It was a huge moment for both teams. Gabriel Jesus made it clear he wanted to take the penalty – as he done previously on several occasions – but Riyad Mahrez felt confident enough to take responsibility. Anfield held its breath as the Algerian ran up – but as his effort blazed over the crossbar, the Blues were left to rue the first real chance to move clear of the Reds with the 0-0 draw preserving both unbeaten records.

City had been patient and measured with the 51% possession the lowest under Pep's reign.

Jurgen Klopp was full of praise for City and was understandably relieved to have taken a point. He said: "It is a very intense, an unbelievable

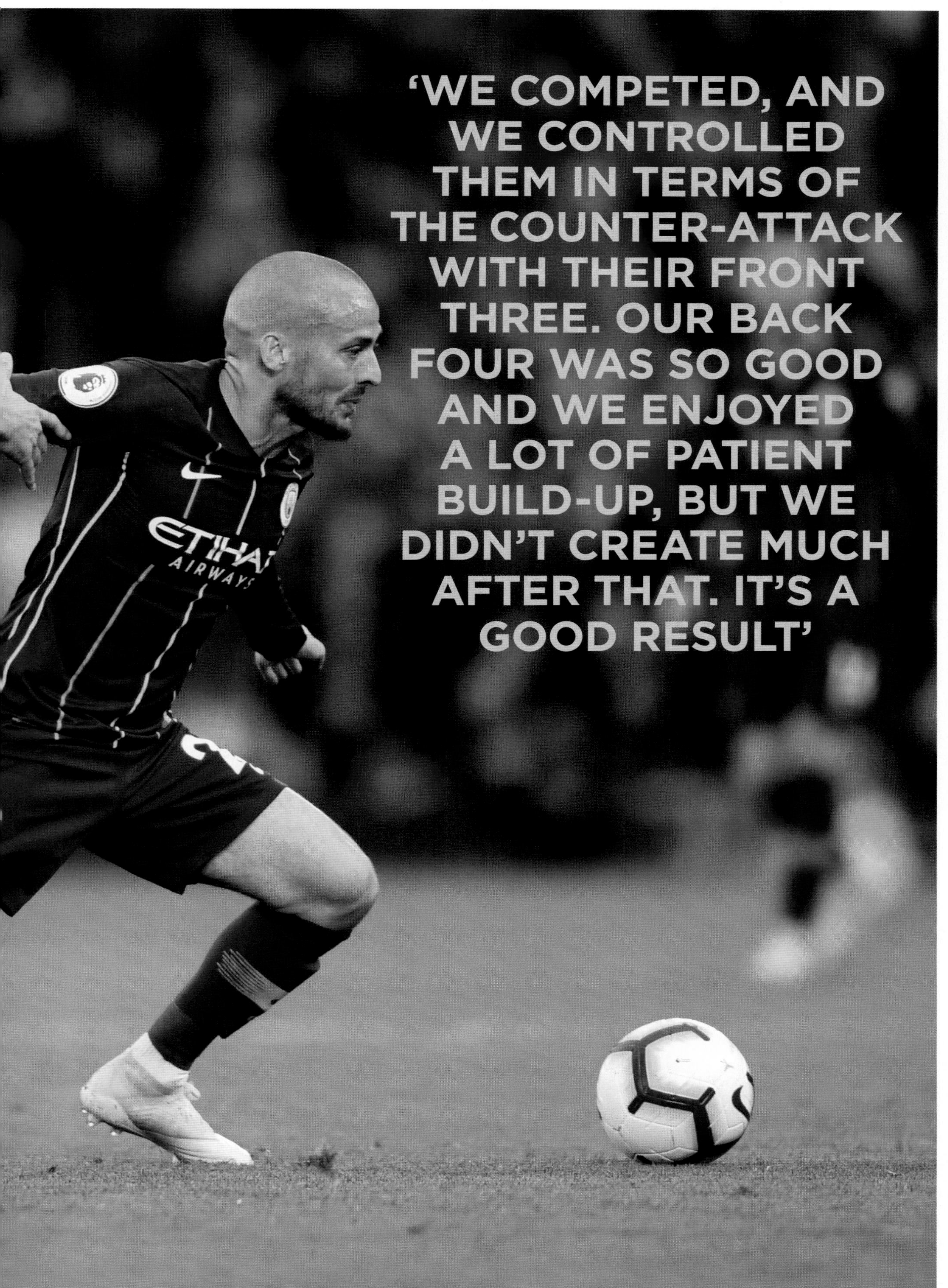

'WE COMPETED, AND WE CONTROLLED THEM IN TERMS OF THE COUNTER-ATTACK WITH THEIR FRONT THREE. OUR BACK FOUR WAS SO GOOD AND WE ENJOYED A LOT OF PATIENT BUILD-UP, BUT WE DIDN'T CREATE MUCH AFTER THAT. IT'S A GOOD RESULT'

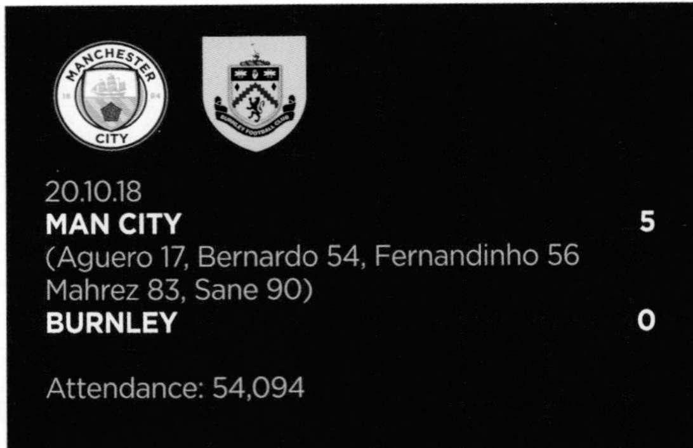

challenge to face Manchester City always – I've said that before – and as the last game of an intense period, it makes the challenge even bigger, so I am really happy with what the boys did. We've played City now that often and they're just outstanding."

Pep added: "We competed, and we controlled them in terms of the counter-attack with their front three. Our back four was so good and we enjoyed a lot of patient build-up, but we didn't create much after that. It's a good result.

"We tried to win, and we didn't concede at Anfield which is quite special. We had our chance and we tried to be ourselves."

Liverpool, quite rightly, felt they'd come through a very difficult run of games intact going into the

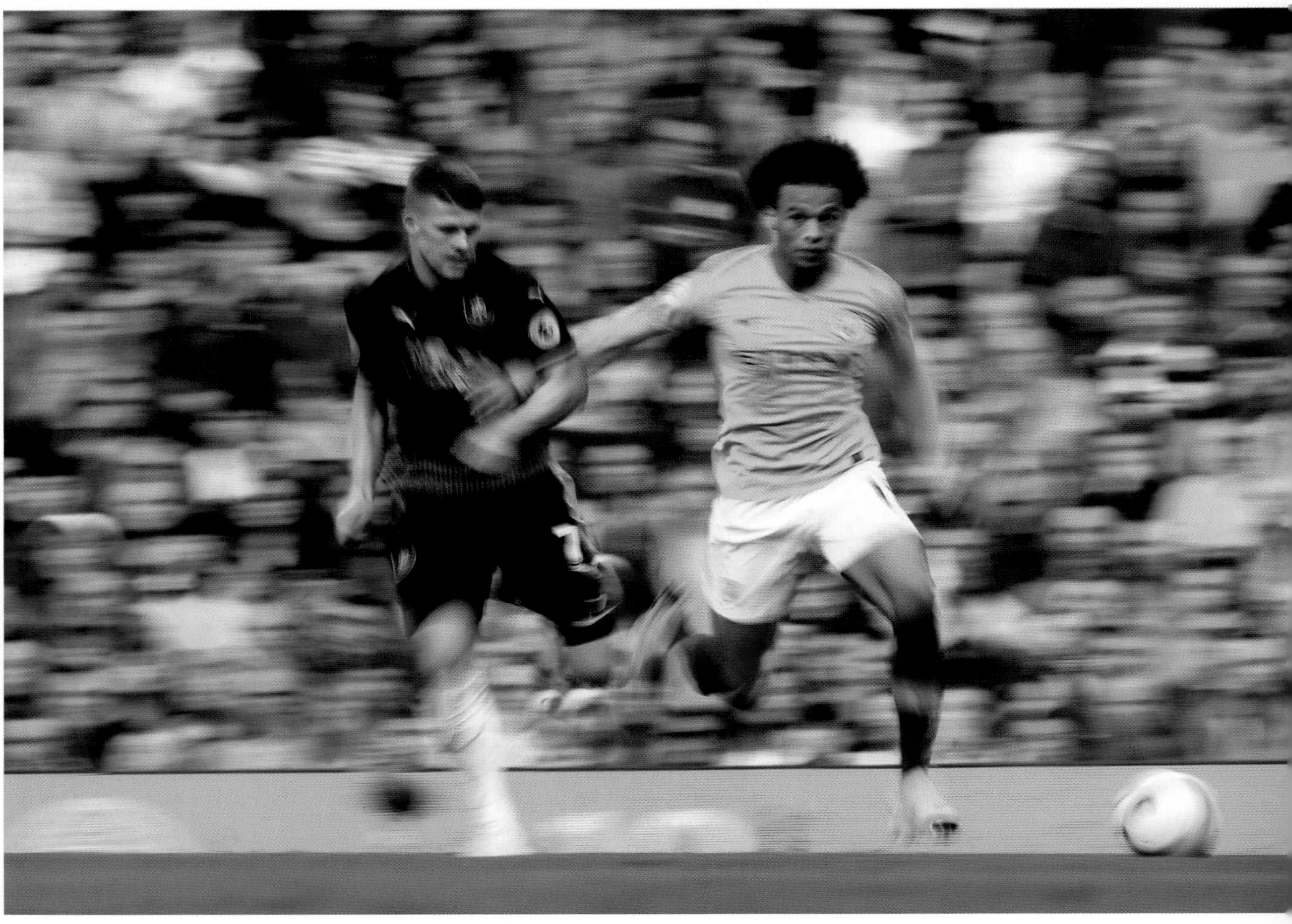

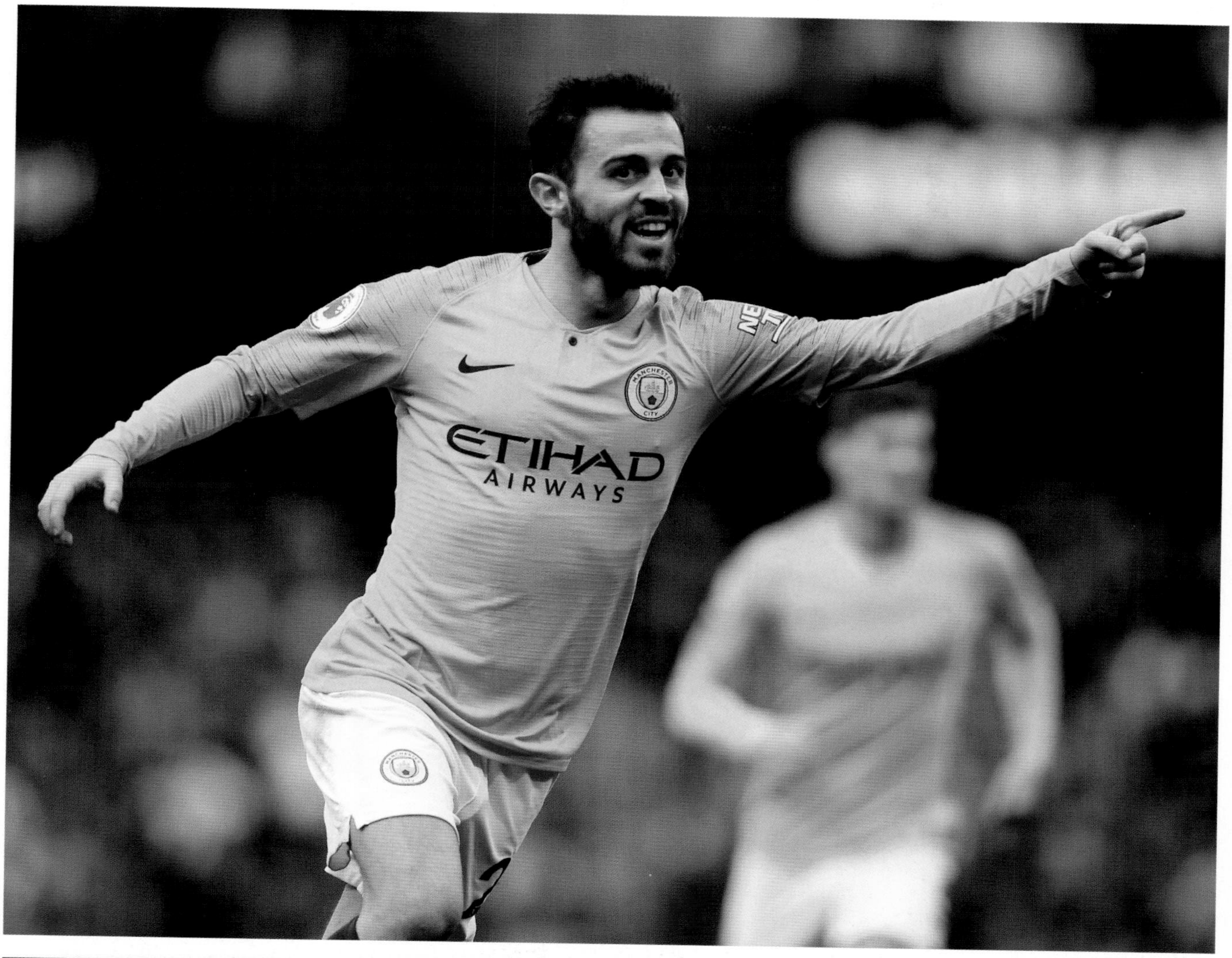
ETIHAD
AIRWAYS

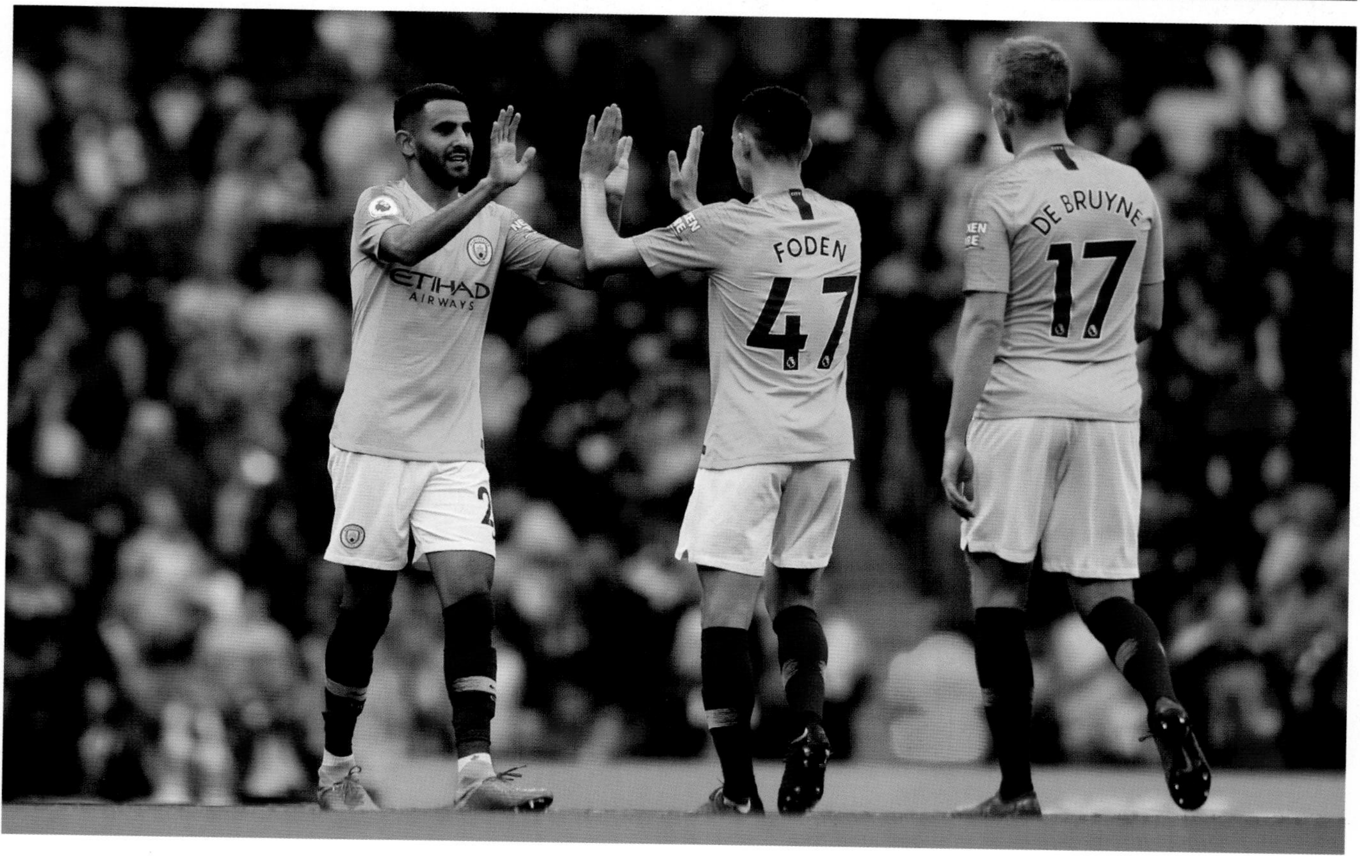
ETIHAD
AIRWAYS
FODEN
47
DE BRUYNE
17

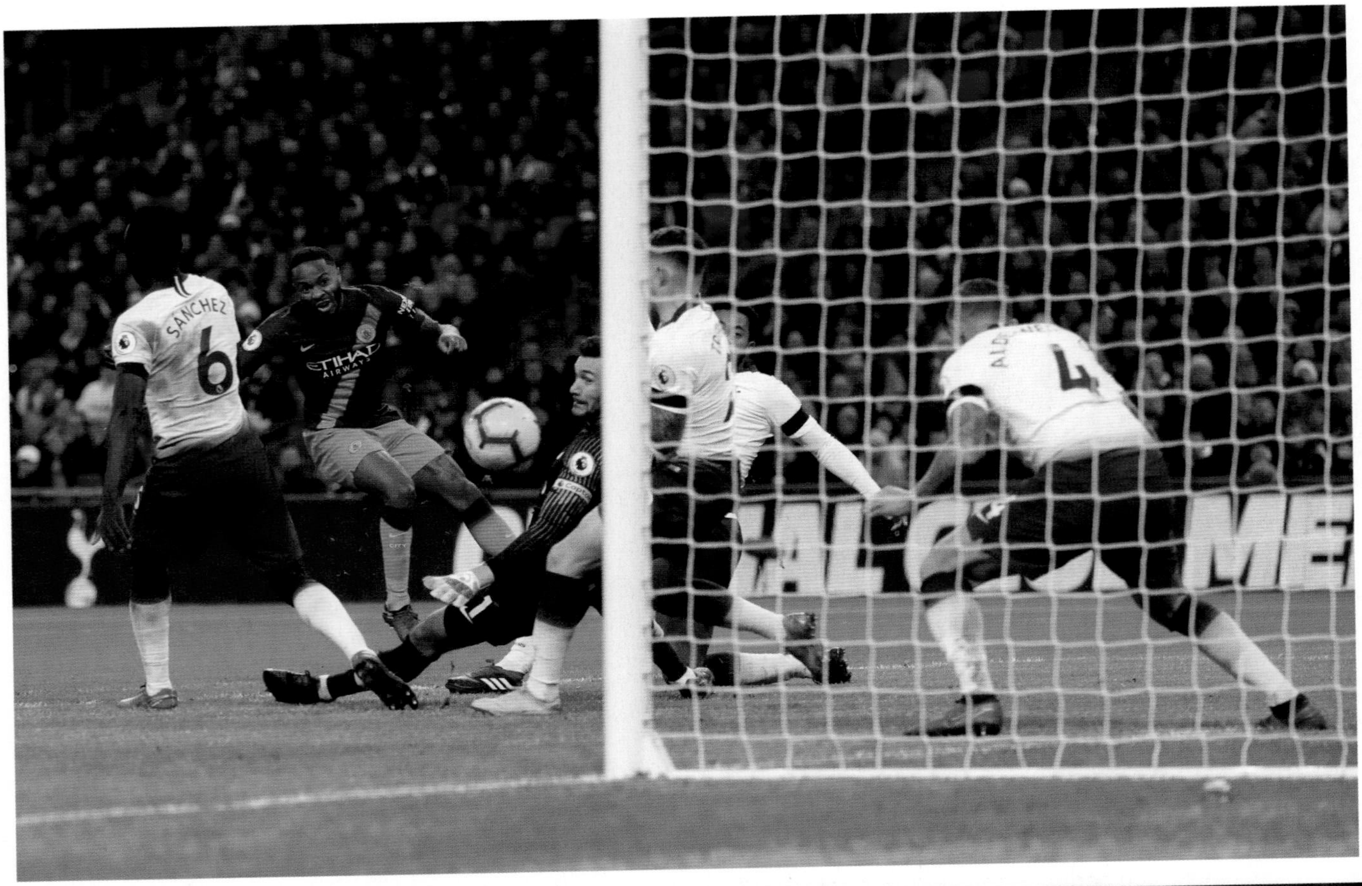

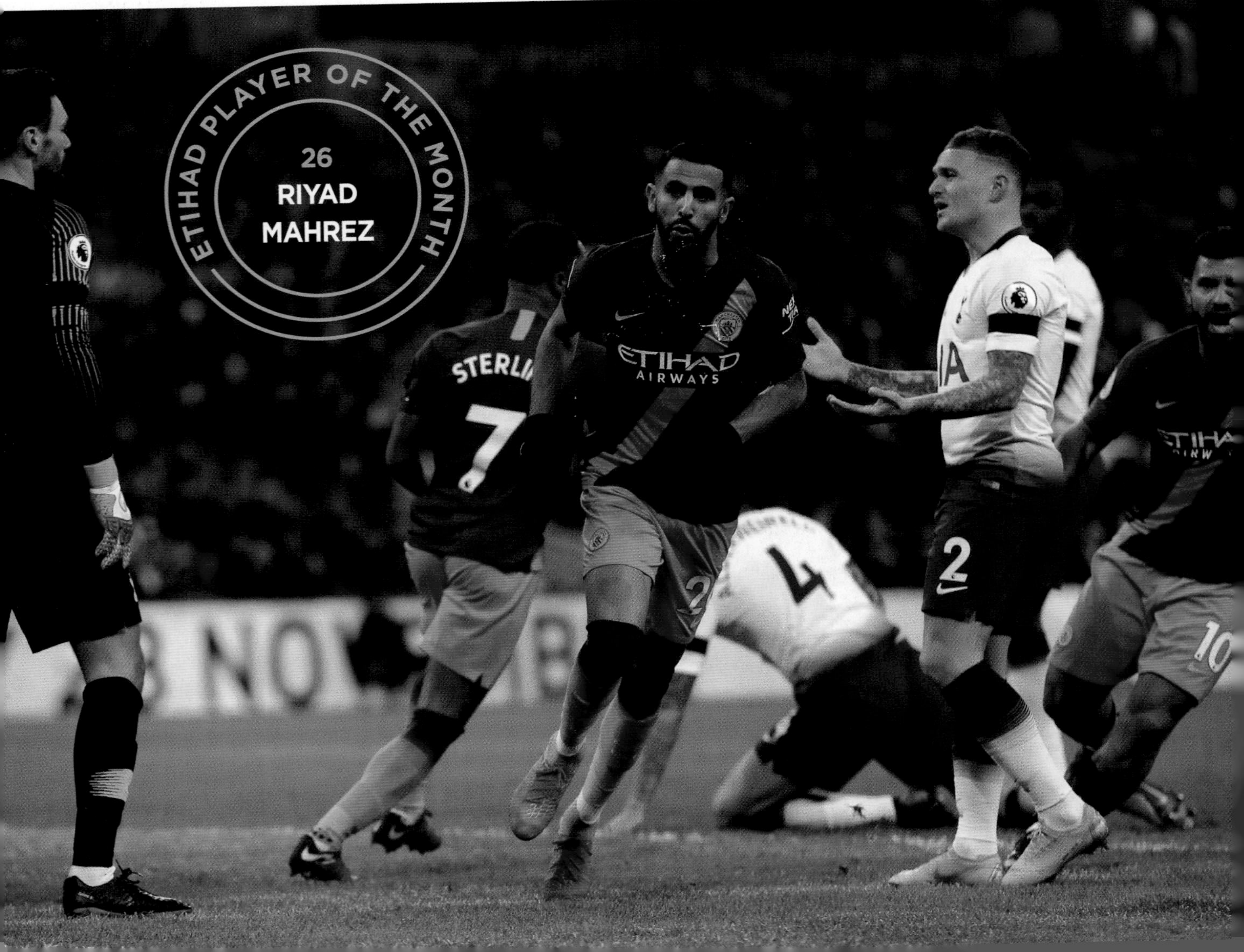

ETIHAD PLAYER OF THE MONTH

26

RIYAD MAHREZ

next international break and while they weren't quite the attacking juggernaut they had been at times the previous campaign, the form of Virgil van Dijk and addition of keeper Allison Becker had made a huge difference to their defence.

The Premier League programme resumed a fortnight later and City kicked off proceedings with a comfortable win over Burnley at the Etihad. If the 5-0 win had been impressive. Liverpool's narrow 1-0 win at Huddersfield was anything but - though it did prove that Klopp's side had found a way to win without playing particularly well.

Liverpool finished the month with a 4-1 win over Cardiff City, with the Blues not in action for another 48 hours with a difficult trip to Wembley to face Tottenham - who could leapfrog the champions into second spot with a victory - still to come. On a pitch that still resembled an NFL field complete with barely disguised markings following a game between Philadelphia Eagles and the Jacksonville Jaguars just 24 hours before, the Blues overcame a poor playing surface to edge a crucial win courtesy of Mahrez's sixth-minute strike.

City remained top going into November, level on points with Liverpool with Chelsea, Arsenal and Spurs all tucked in close behind and Bournemouth in the sixth. In fact, just six points separated the top six with 10 games played - the Blues had already been five points clear at the top at this stage the previous season and, tellingly, 12 ahead of Liverpool. It was fascinating stuff.

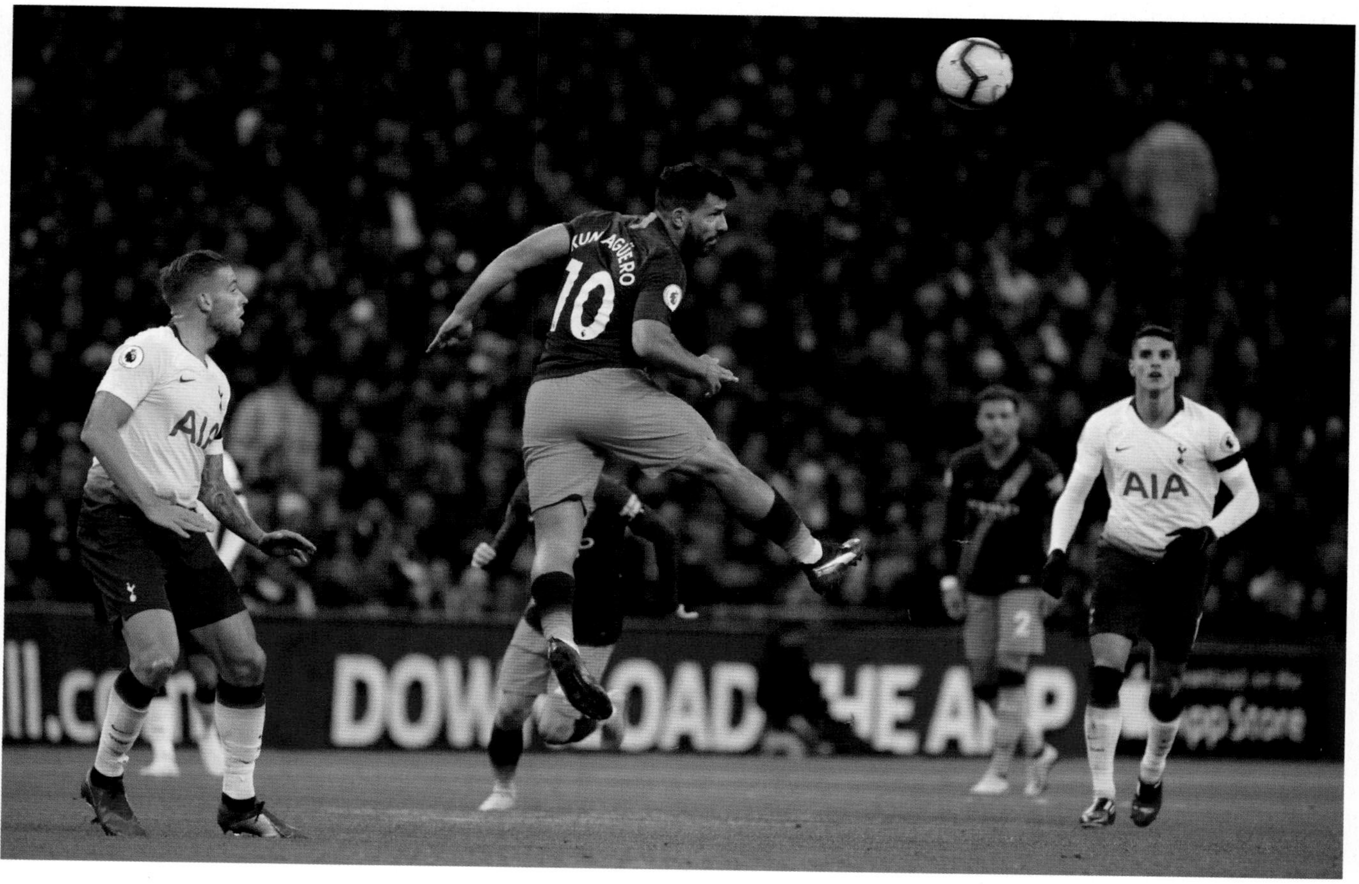

GOALS GALORE

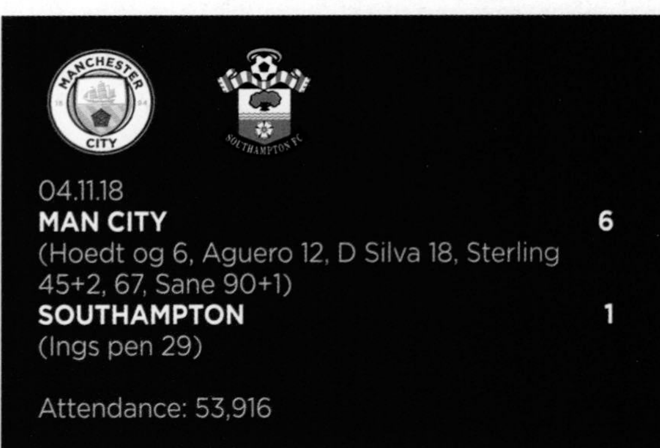

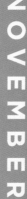

04.11.18
MAN CITY 6
(Hoedt og 6, Aguero 12, D Silva 18, Sterling 45+2, 67, Sane 90+1)
SOUTHAMPTON 1
(Ings pen 29)

Attendance: 53,916

November started well for City as Liverpool dropped two points in their 0-0 draw with Arsenal and with the game coming 24 hours earlier than City's game at home to Southampton.

The previous year it had taken a Raheem Sterling winner deep into added time to see off the Saints 2-1, but there was no such problem this time as City raced into a 4-1 lead at the break, going on to win 6-1.

A Wesley Hoedt own goal plus strikes from David Silva, Sergio Aguero, Sterling (2) and Leroy Sane did the damage and as a result, the

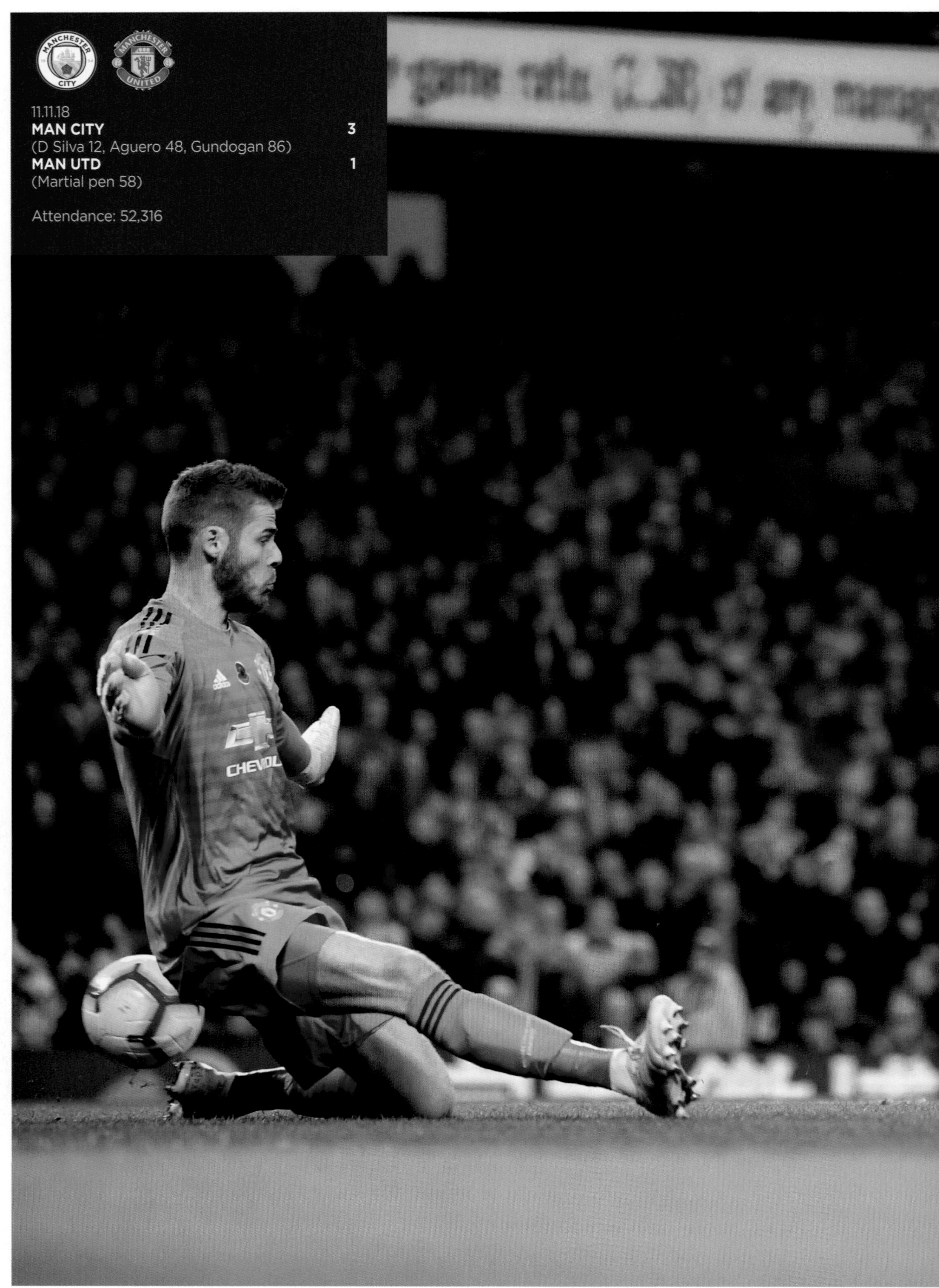

11.11.18

MAN CITY 3

(D Silva 12, Aguero 48, Gundogan 86)

MAN UTD 1

(Martial pen 58)

Attendance: 52,316

Blues moved two points clear of second-placed Chelsea and Liverpool.

Neither City, Chelsea or Liverpool were showing signs of fragility and the chasing pack had begun to take points off each other. City went into the Manchester derby full of confidence with a thumping drive from Aguero and two Ilkay Gundogan goals seeing off Jose Mourinho's side 3-1 at the Etihad.

The rampant Blues then thrashed West Ham at the London Stadium, racing into a three-goal lead with just 34 minutes played before going on to add another after half-time in a comfortable 4-0 win. City had every right to feel there should now be some breathing space at the top of the Premier League, but Liverpool beat Fulham 2-0 at Anfield and Watford 3-0 at Vicarage Road to stay right on the champions' shoulder.

Tottenham were hanging in there in third spot, just five points off top spot but Chelsea were starting to fall away somewhat. For neutrals, however it was all about the battle between City and Liverpool – two teams, focused, defensively strong and blessed with free-scoring attacks going neck and neck for the ultimate prize in domestic football.

For City, however, December would be anything but magic...

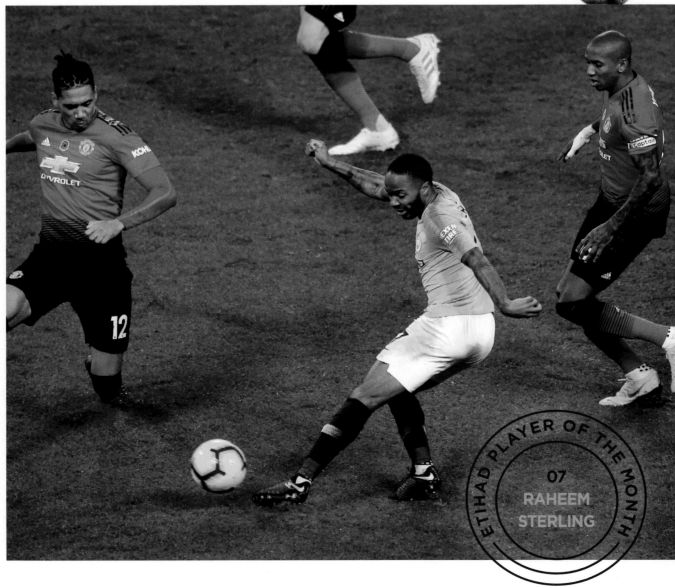

ETIHAD PLAYER OF THE MONTH

07

RAHEEM STERLING

12
SMALLING
27
FELLAINI
31
MATIC
5
STONES
18

NEXEN
TIRE
10

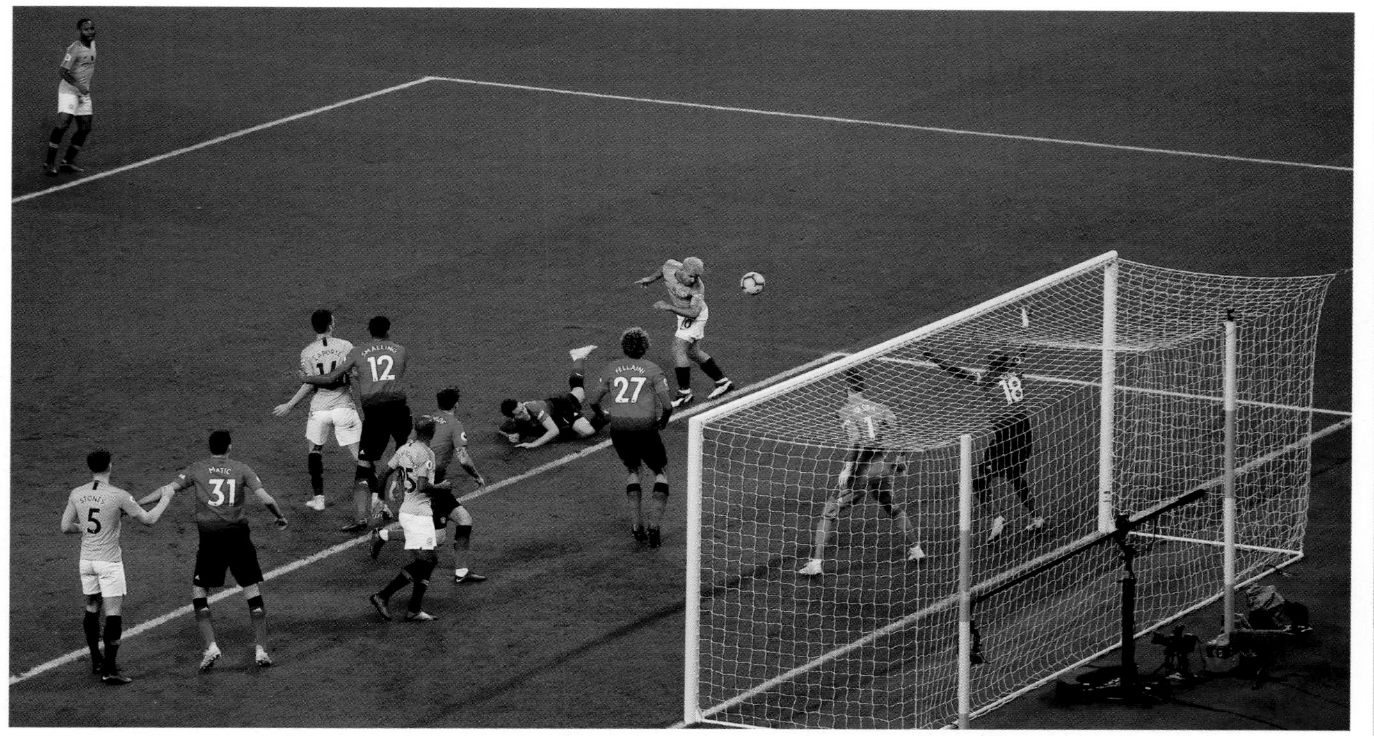

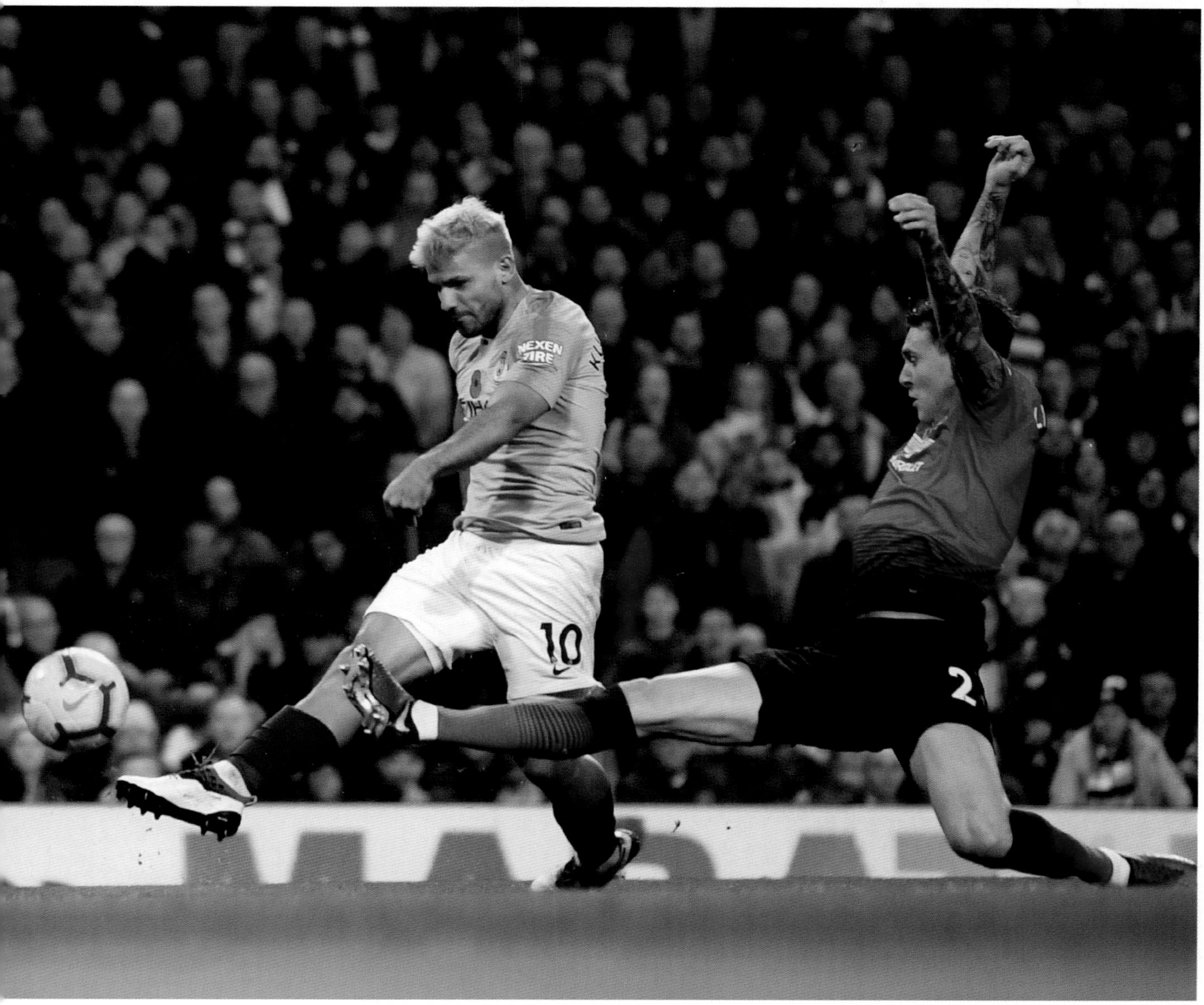

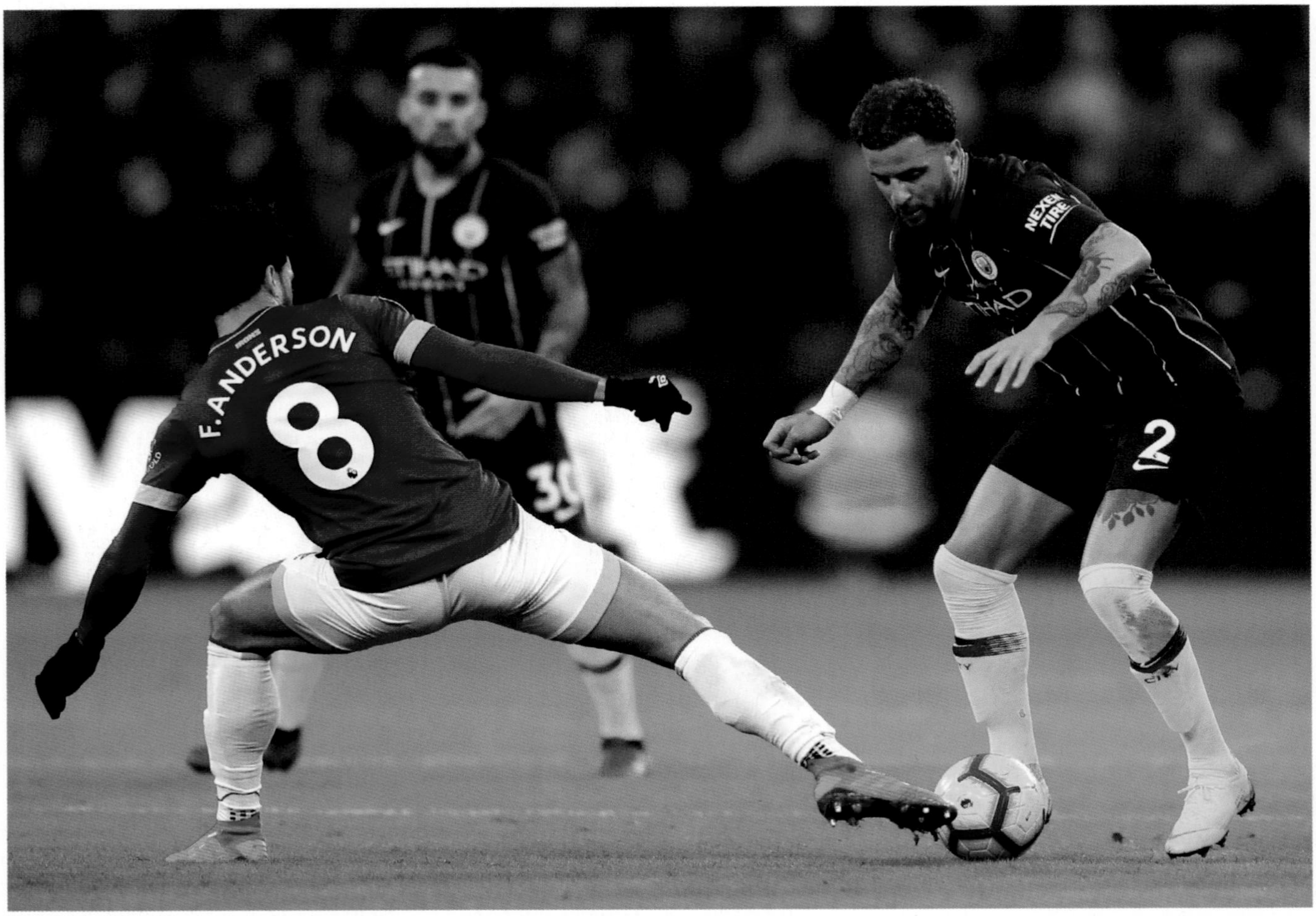
F. ANDERSON
8
NEXEN TIRE
2

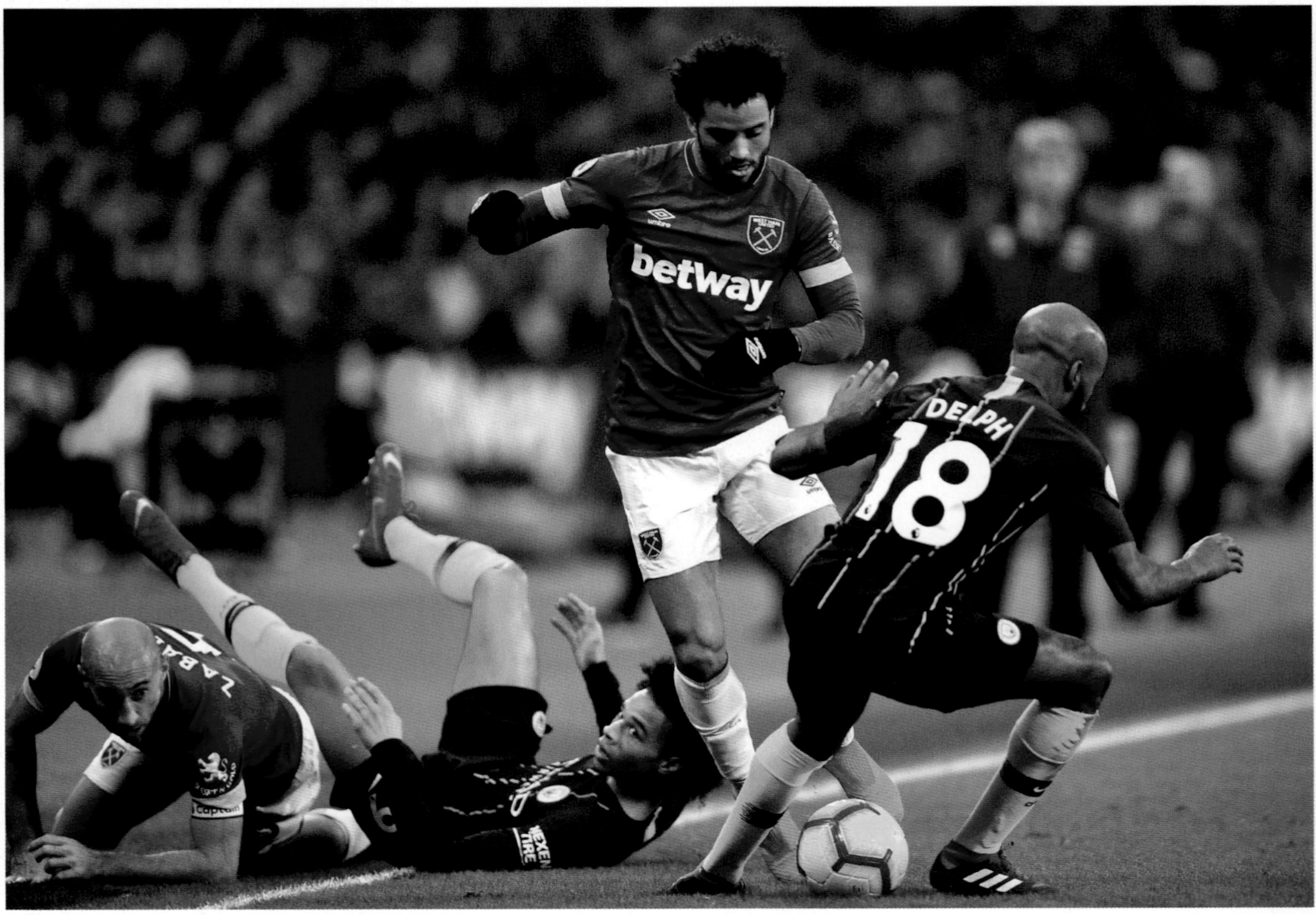
betway
DELPH
18
NEXEN TIRE
Captain

NOVEMBER

24.11.18

WEST HAM 0

MAN CITY 4

(Silva 11, Sterling 19, Sane 34, 90+3)

Attendance: 56,886

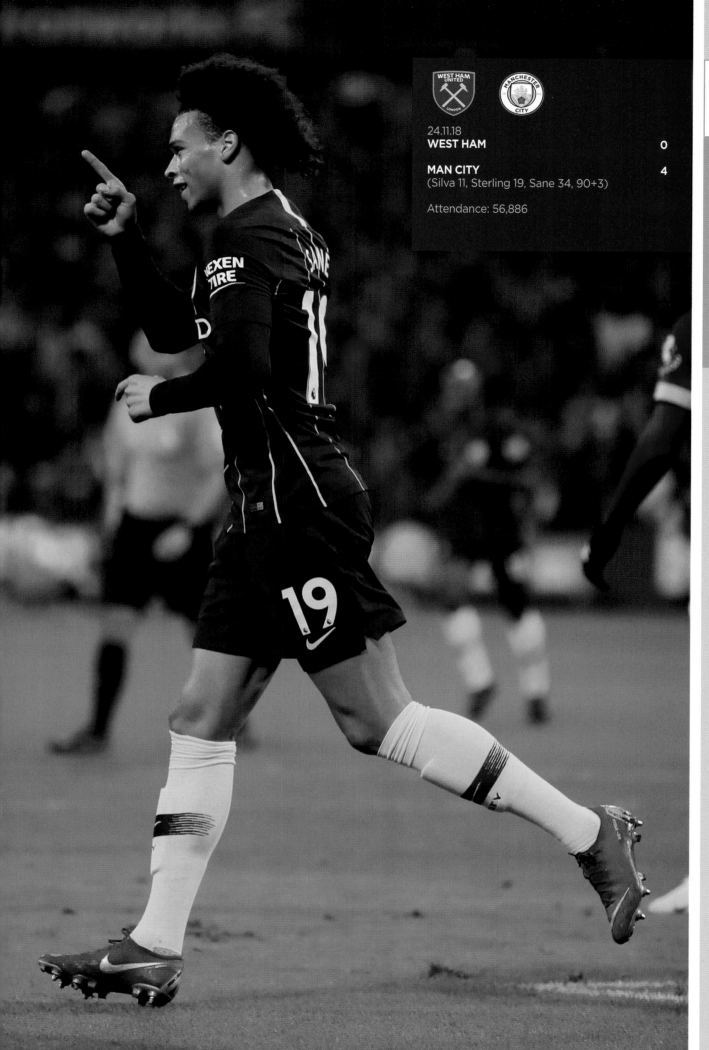

WINTER BLUES

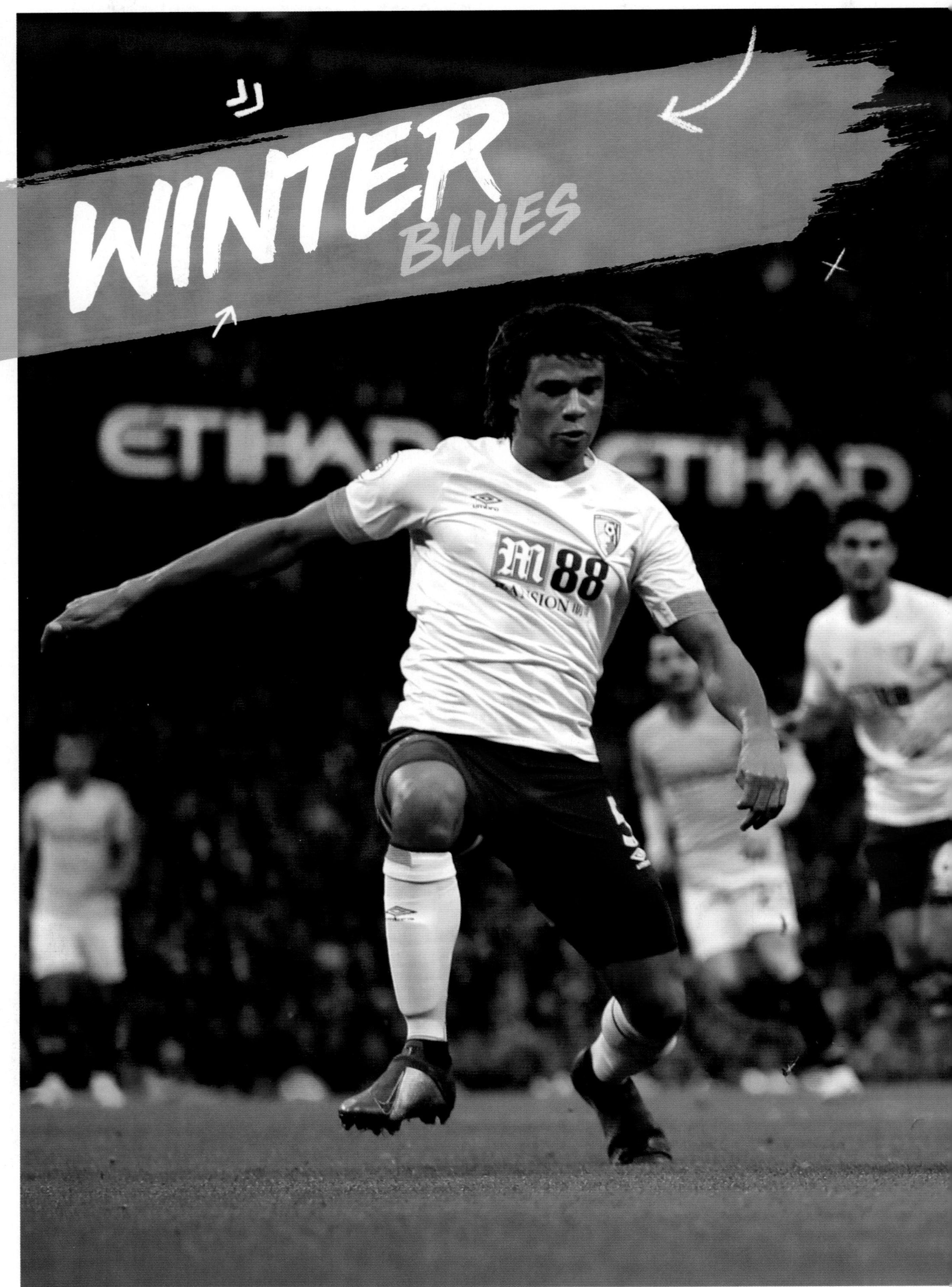

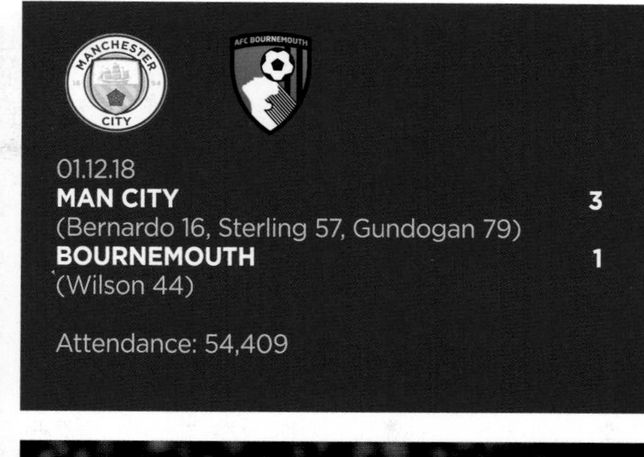

01.12.18
MAN CITY 3
(Bernardo 16, Sterling 57, Gundogan 79)
BOURNEMOUTH 1
(Wilson 44)

Attendance: 54,409

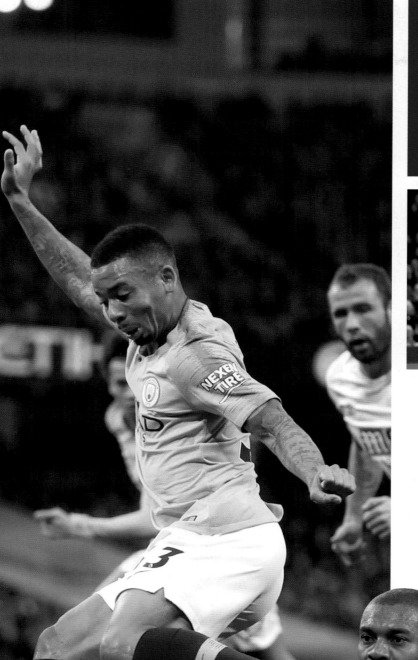

The Blues kicked off December with a fairly straightforward 3-1 win over Bournemouth with Bernardo, Raheem Sterling and Ilkay Gundogan all on target. City fans then settled down to watch the Merseyside derby, hoping the Toffees could grind out a result and knock Liverpool out of their stride. Though Everton's record at Anfield was poor, the Toffees frustrated Klopp's side and as the game moved into added time still goalless, it looked like Liverpool would again drop vital points, this time to their nearest rivals.

But on 96 minutes, van Dijk's hopeful punt looked set to go into touch until it was inexplicably pawed into play by Everton keeper Jordan Pickford, allowing sub Divock Origi the simplest of headers to win the game. It's fair to say a few TV remotes were hurled across the room at that point as the growing belief that Liverpool were in for the long haul grew with each passing game.

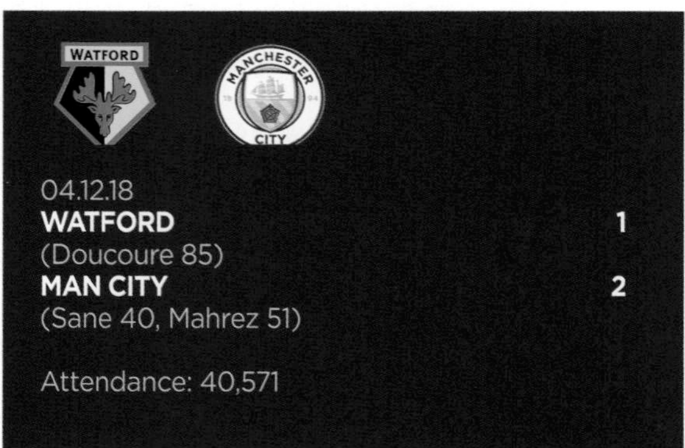

WATFORD
04.12.18
WATFORD 1
(Doucoure 85)
MAN CITY 2
(Sane 40, Mahrez 51)
Attendance: 40,571

City next endured a tricky end to what had otherwise been a comfortable midweek visit to Watford, clinging on to win 2-1 after a late onslaught from the Hornets and, crucially, go five points clear of Liverpool for at least 24 hours. The Reds again reduced the arrears the following day, coming from behind to beat Burnley 3-1 at Turf Moor.

As Christmas approached, the Blues - still in all four competitions - had their first real set-back of the season. Two, in fact. The first damaging blow landed came at Stamford Bridge, where - despite an excellent first 45 minutes where City arguably played some of their best football to date - fell behind on the stroke of half-time to Ngolo Kante's thunderous goal. Chelsea added a second late on to secure a 2-0 win and end the Blues' unbeaten start to the season and a 21-game unbeaten Premier League run. Liverpool seized the initiative with a 4-0 win at Bournemouth to

TAND
FxPro
FxPro

go top, but things were about to get worse for the champions. Much worse.

Though the next game City beat Everton 3-1 at the Etihad, Liverpool also won, beating Manchester United by the same score-line to maintain their slender advantage. The Reds also played their next game 24 hours earlier than the Blues and confidently dispatched Wolves 2-0 at Molineux to move four points clear at the top.

Jurgen Klopp said his team were playing "perfect football" and City, at home to struggling Crystal Palace, had to respond. When Ilkay Gundogan's header on 27 minutes put the Blues ahead, there seemed little doubt that the Blues would go on and win comfortably, but just eight minutes later, Palace had turned the game on its head and were 2-1 up, the second goal an

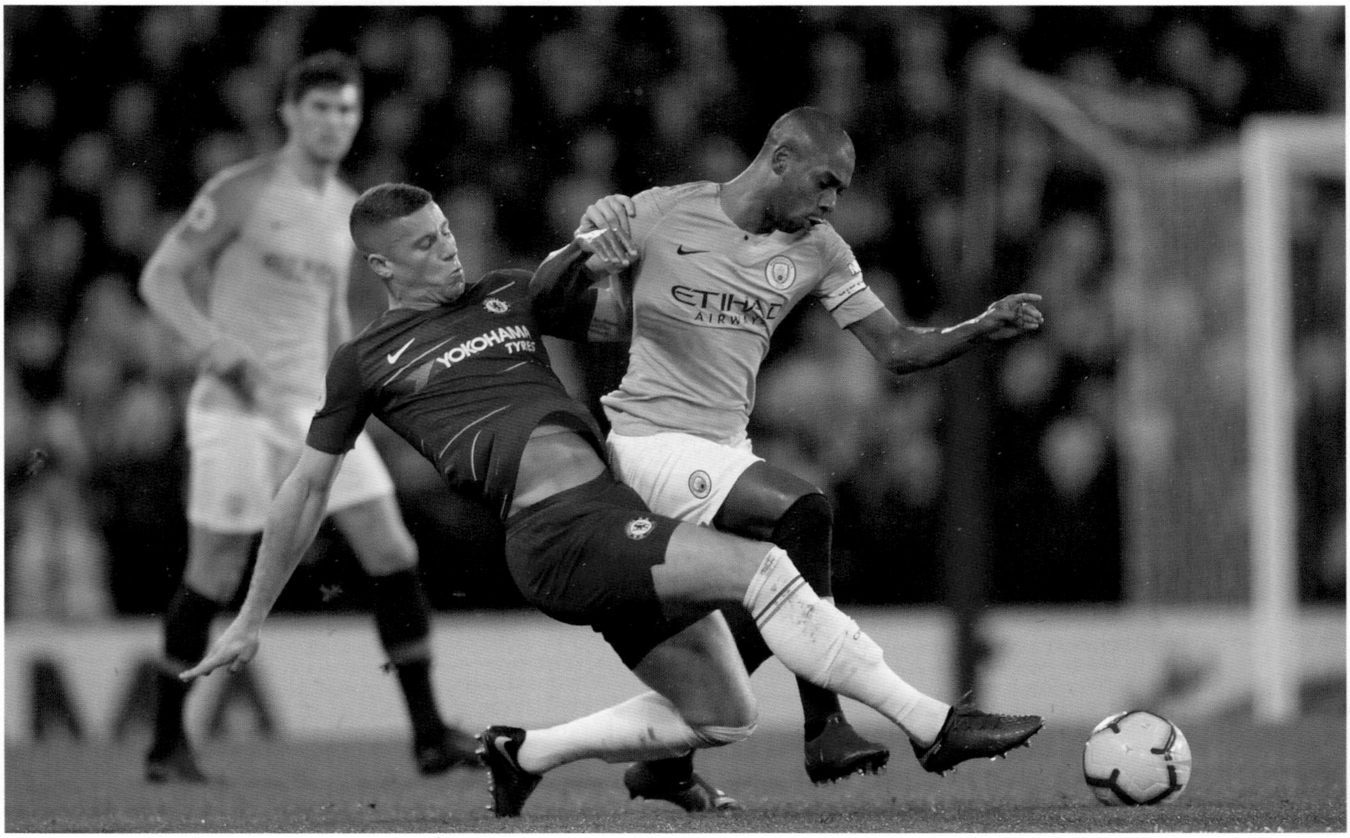

15.12.18

MAN CITY (Jesus 22, 50, Sterling 69)	3
EVERTON (Calvert-Lewin 65)	1

Attendance: 54,173

absolute stunner from Andros Townsend who volleyed an unstoppable shot from more than 30 yards out.

Worse was to come as the lively Palace belied their lowly position with a third from the penalty spot on 52 minutes following a clumsy Kyle Walker challenge. Kevin De Bruyne, absent for most of the campaign with a knee injury, pulled a late goal back but Palace held on to win 3-2 and send shockwaves throughout the Premier League and beyond. Not only had Roy Hodgson's side beaten City, they had done so on merit and in the champions' own backyard.

An instant response was needed and the Boxing Day trip to Leicester provided the opportunity to do exactly that. Both City and Liverpool kicked off at 3pm, but while the Blues suddenly looked a little vulnerable and edgy, so Liverpool looked invigorated, determined to grasp the opportunity Palace had given them - and Klopp's side didn't disappoint their fans as they swept Rafa Benitez's Newcastle aside with a 4-0 win at Anfield.

Meanwhile, the Blues had taken the initiative at the King Power with Bernardo Silva's 14th-minute strike, but the Foxes, sniffing blood and a rarely seen apprehensiveness from City, soon levelled and Ricardo Pereira's late winner completed a miserable festive period for the champions who now trailed Liverpool by seven points - a gap, that suddenly felt as wide as the Mersey tunnel.

Pep admitted his team was suffering when he said: "It was a similar performance to the Crystal Palace game, we started well but conceded a goal the first time they arrived in our box. Mentally we are lacking confidence in

ETIHAD PLAYER OF THE MONTH

20
BERNARDO
SILVA

22.12.18
MAN CITY 2
(Gundogan 27, De Bruyne 85)
CRYSTAL PALACE 3
(Schlupp 33, Townsend 35, Milivojevic pen 51)

Attendance: 54,340

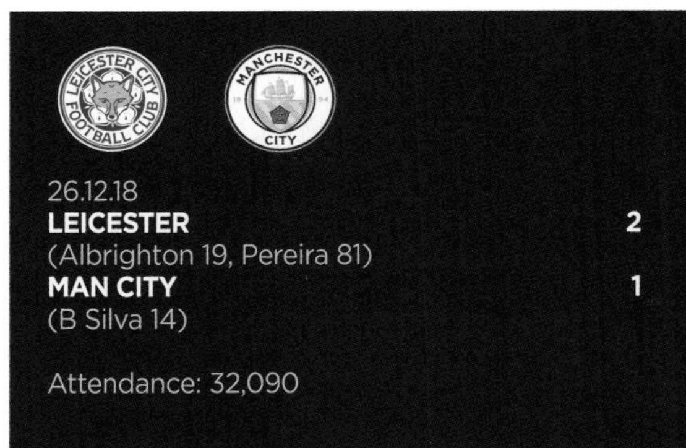

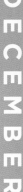

26.12.18
LEICESTER 2
(Albrighton 19, Pereira 81)
MAN CITY 1
(B Silva 14)

Attendance: 32,090

that situation. We have to accept it; we have to realise that we have to work harder and try to get immediately one good result and get our confidence back."

City knew another slip would probably be a bridge too far - even with half the campaign still to go - and so headed to Southampton needing to end the year with nothing less than a victory, but the pressure on the champions had never been more intense, particularly after Liverpool's 5-1 thrashing of Arsenal had increased their lead at the top to 10 points ahead of the clash at St Mary's.

The Blues boss was confident his team would deliver and put what had been a severe hiccup behind them - and by the break, City were proving him right, leading Saints 3-1, even if the display hadn't been vintage City. There would be no further goals, the gap was reduced to seven points and the first fixture of the New Year was Liverpool at home, where nothing less than a victory would do for the Blues - 2019 had to begin with three points or there would surely be no way back for Pep's men.

30.12.18
SOUTHAMPTON 1
(Hojbjerg 37)
MAN CITY 3
(Silva 10, Ward-Prowse og 45, Aguero 45+3)

Attendance: 31,381

SUMMIT MEETING

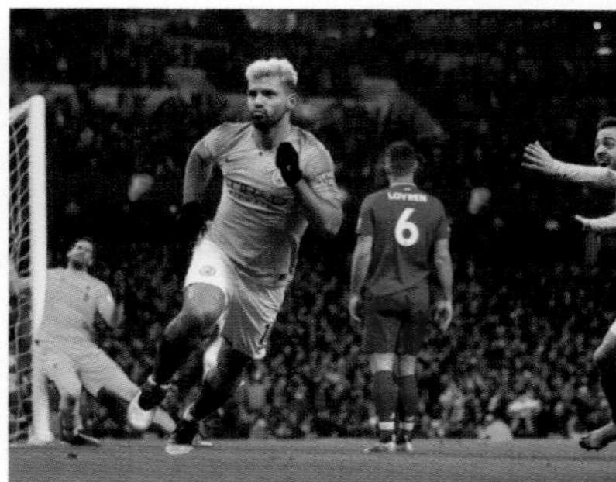

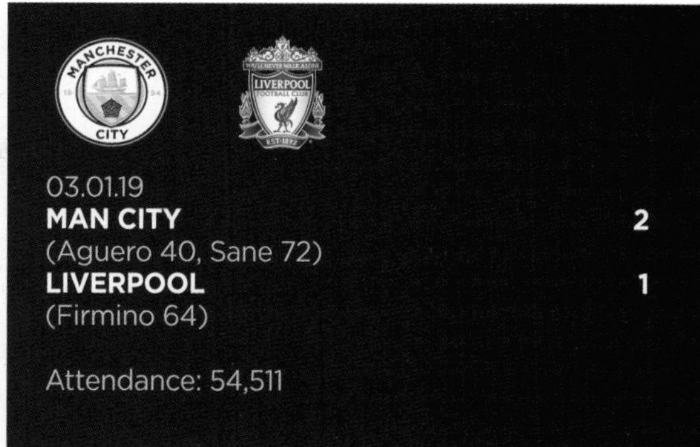

03.01.19
MAN CITY 2
(Aguero 40, Sane 72)
LIVERPOOL 1
(Firmino 64)

Attendance: 54,511

There was tension, nerves and anxiety in the air as City and Liverpool walked out at the Etihad for their latest titanic tussle. It wasn't winner takes all, but it felt like the result of this encounter would have a huge bearing on the title race.

For the Blues, a victory would not only end the Merseysiders' unbeaten start, it would reduce the gap to the leaders to just four – a loss for City would see a surely insurmountable 10-point advantage for Klopp's side with only 17 games remaining.

If Pep felt his team had been mentally fragile towards the end of December, they were anything but for this tense blood and thunder contest in a game of genuinely fine margins. Liverpool almost went ahead when Sadio Mane's scuffed effort hit the post, the ball was cleared against Ederson and was rolling towards the empty net when John Stones somehow hooked his foot around it to clear the danger – the goal-line technology suggested the ball had been a couple of millimetres short of being given as a goal and City survived. The first goal would be crucial and it was City who broke the deadlock when Sergio Aguero fired an angled shot past Allison just before the break to send the Etihad into raptures.

The contest, however, was far from over and after a spell of sustained pressure, Roberto Firmino levelled on 64 minutes to keep the match finely balanced. It felt like Liverpool suddenly had the momentum, but City dug deep, stood strong and on 79 minutes, Leroy Sane's low shot beat Allison and went in off the post to once again send the Etihad wild. The relief was palpable, and the Blues held out to win 2-1. Instead of 10 points, Liverpool's lead at the top was now just four – a six-pointer if ever there was!

Afterwards, Pep said: "All credit to these incredible players. Both teams tried to search for each other, we were not scared, we had no fear and we had a lot of pressure. They are leaders but we have reduced the gap. We knew that if we won, we would be in contention to fight for the Premier League, if we lose it is over. I don't remember a league so tough, there are so many huge contenders fighting for the title. Every game is a final."

If Liverpool had got under City's skin before, this was a result that left the Reds wondering 'what if?' Suddenly, it was game on again. City followed the victory with successive 3-0 wins over Wolves and Huddersfield, while Liverpool held their nerve with a 1-0 win at Brighton and 4-3 win over Crystal Palace at Anfield where a couple of goalkeeping howlers from visiting keeper Julian Speroni were not warmly received in the blue half of Manchester.

14.01.19
MAN CITY 3
(Gabriel Jesus 10, pen 39, Coady og 78)
WOLVES 0
Attendance: 54,171

20.01.19

HUDDERSFIELD 0

MANCHESTER CITY 3
(Danilo 18, Sterling 54, Sane 56)

Attendance: 24,190

ETIHAD
AIRWAYS

ETIHAD
AIRWAYS

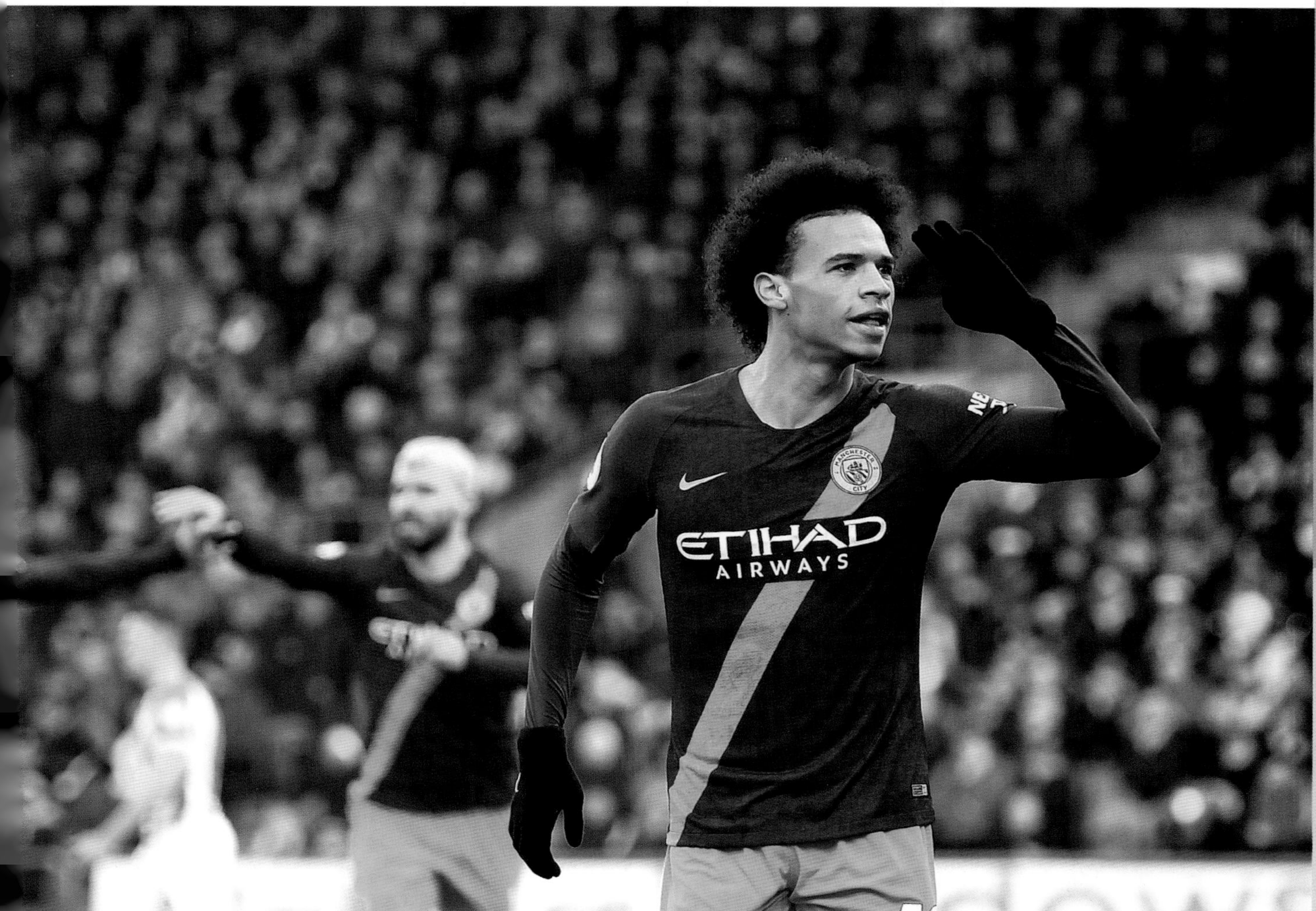

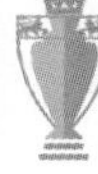

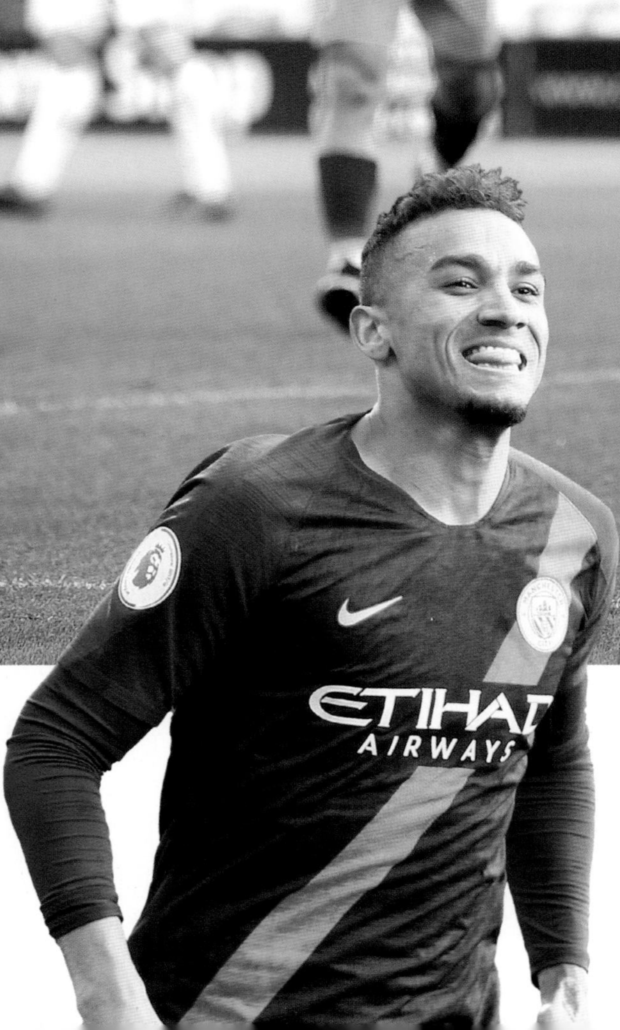

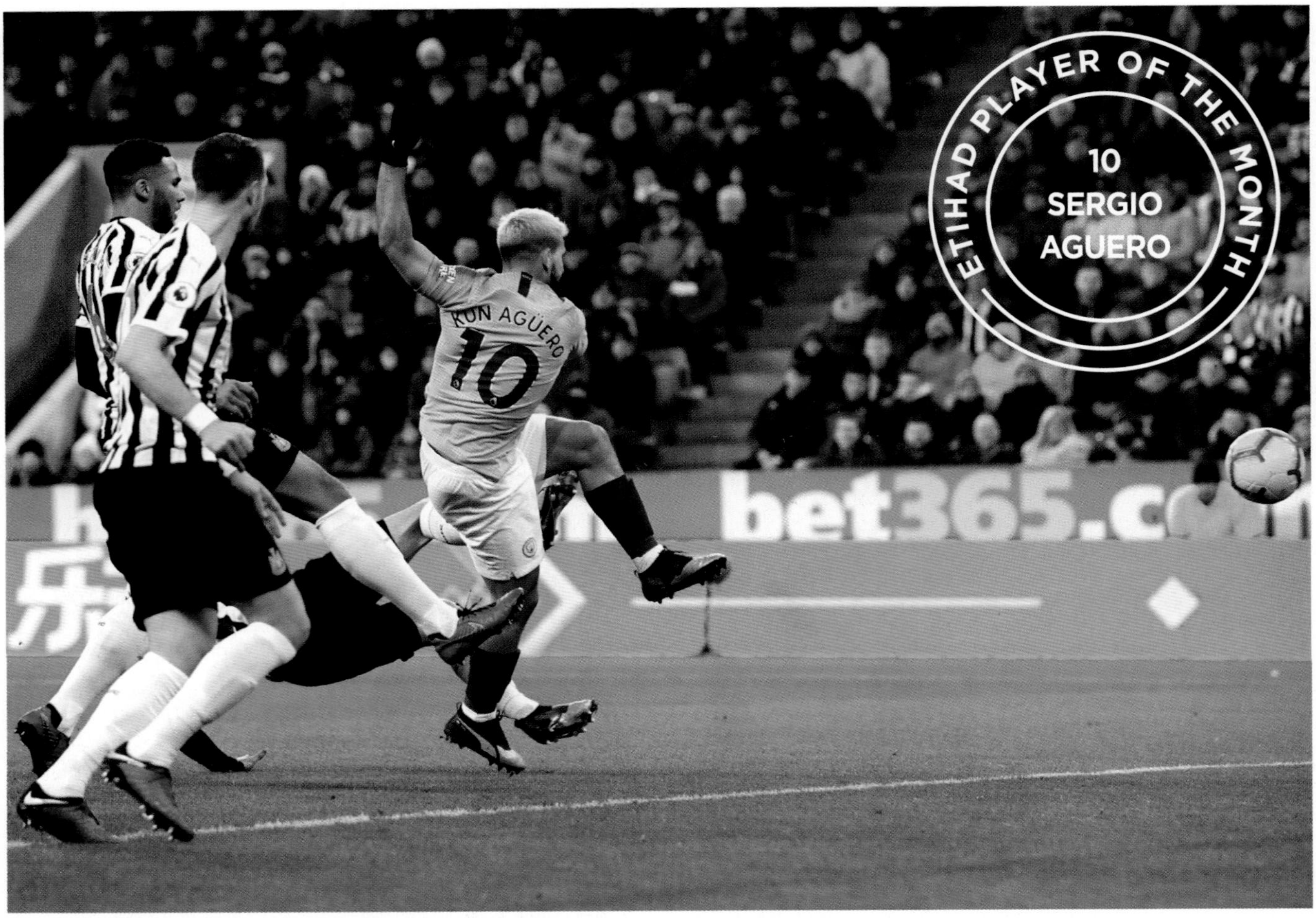

ETIHAD PLAYER OF THE MONTH

10
SERGIO
AGUERO

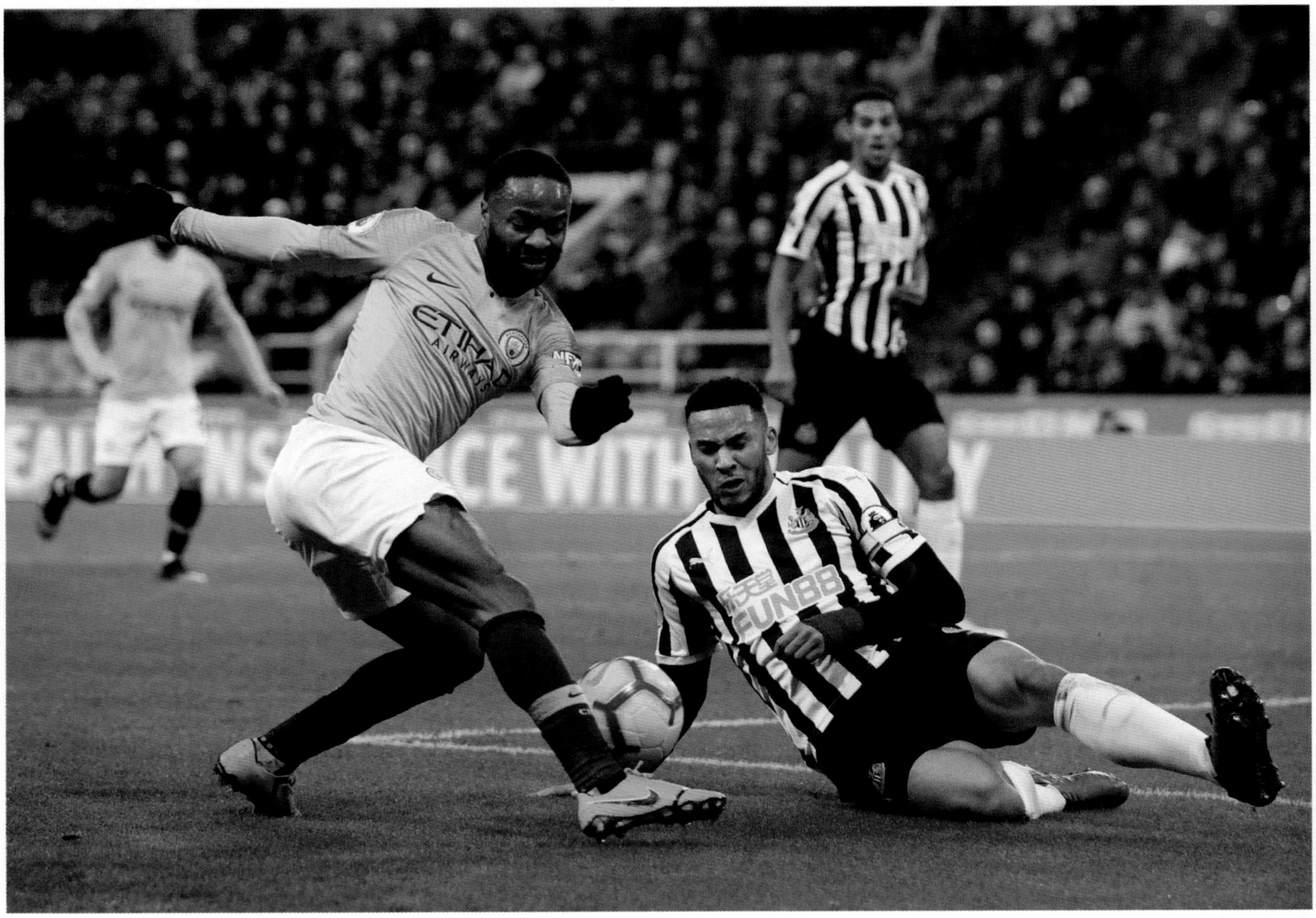

Next up, the Blues had the chance to move within a point of Liverpool with a game against Newcastle 24 hours before the Reds hosted Leicester. City could hardly have started better on Tyneside, taking the lead after just 24 seconds through Aguero, but the failure to capitalise on that flying start allowed the Magpies' belief to grow and when Salomon Rondon levelled on 66 minutes, the doubt that had surfaced around Christmas seemed to re-emerge. With 10 minutes to play Fernandinho's challenge resulted in a late penalty, converted by Matt Ritchie to give the Magpies a 2-1 win and end a long losing streak against the champions.

After working so hard to get back in the title race, had the Blues now shot themselves in the foot?

It would be 24 hours later before we would find out – could the misfiring Leicester really pull off a surprise at Anfield? Surely Klopp's side wouldn't miss the chance to reassert a seven-point gap? When Sadio Mane opened the scoring after three minutes, it seemed not – but Leicester held on, dug in and gradually started to claw their way back into the game and, on half-time, Harry Maguire levelled the scores. If City had shown apprehension, now it was Liverpool's turn and by the end of the game, the Foxes were unlucky not to have taken all three points, instead leaving with a damaging 1-1 draw. Klopp said later: "We have a point more than before – it is not exactly what we wanted to have, but still everything is fine."

It must have been worrying for the former Borussia Dortmund boss that his team had not only let City off once, they'd now done it again and while a five-point gap was something Liverpool would have happily accepted going into February, there must have been a feeling that the Blues were not going to keep stuttering as this thrilling Premier League title race continued.

29.01.19

NEWCASTLE 2

(Rondon 66, Ritchie pen 80)

MANCHESTER CITY 1

(Aguero 1)

Attendance: 50,861

NO ROOM FOR ERROR

If December and January had taught City anything, it was that there was no more margin for error. Twice Liverpool could have gone 10 points ahead, once they could have gone eight clear, but none of those chances was taken. There could be no more slip-ups. With 14 games remaining, Pep Guardiola was convinced his team would need to win every one of them – a feat no team had ever managed on the season run-in.

City's game with Arsenal took place 24 hours before Liverpool's trip to West Ham as the rest of the nation waited to see what the next twist in this fascinating title race would be. A 3-1 win, courtesy of a Sergio Aguero hat-trick saw off the Gunners and the gap was – for the time being – back down to just two points, but if this was a

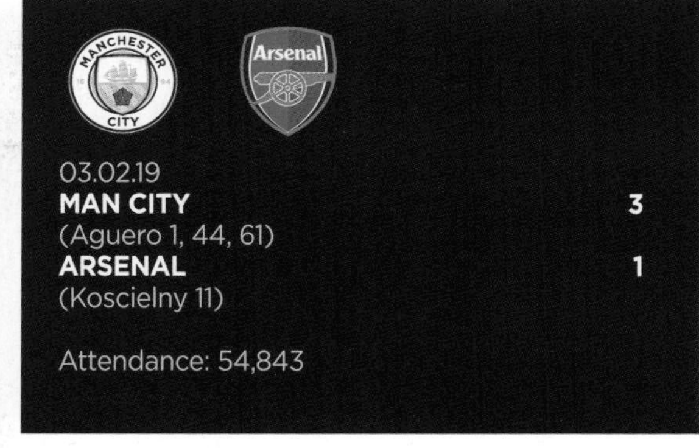

03.02.19

MAN CITY 3

(Aguero 1, 44, 61)

ARSENAL 1

(Koscielny 11)

Attendance: 54,843

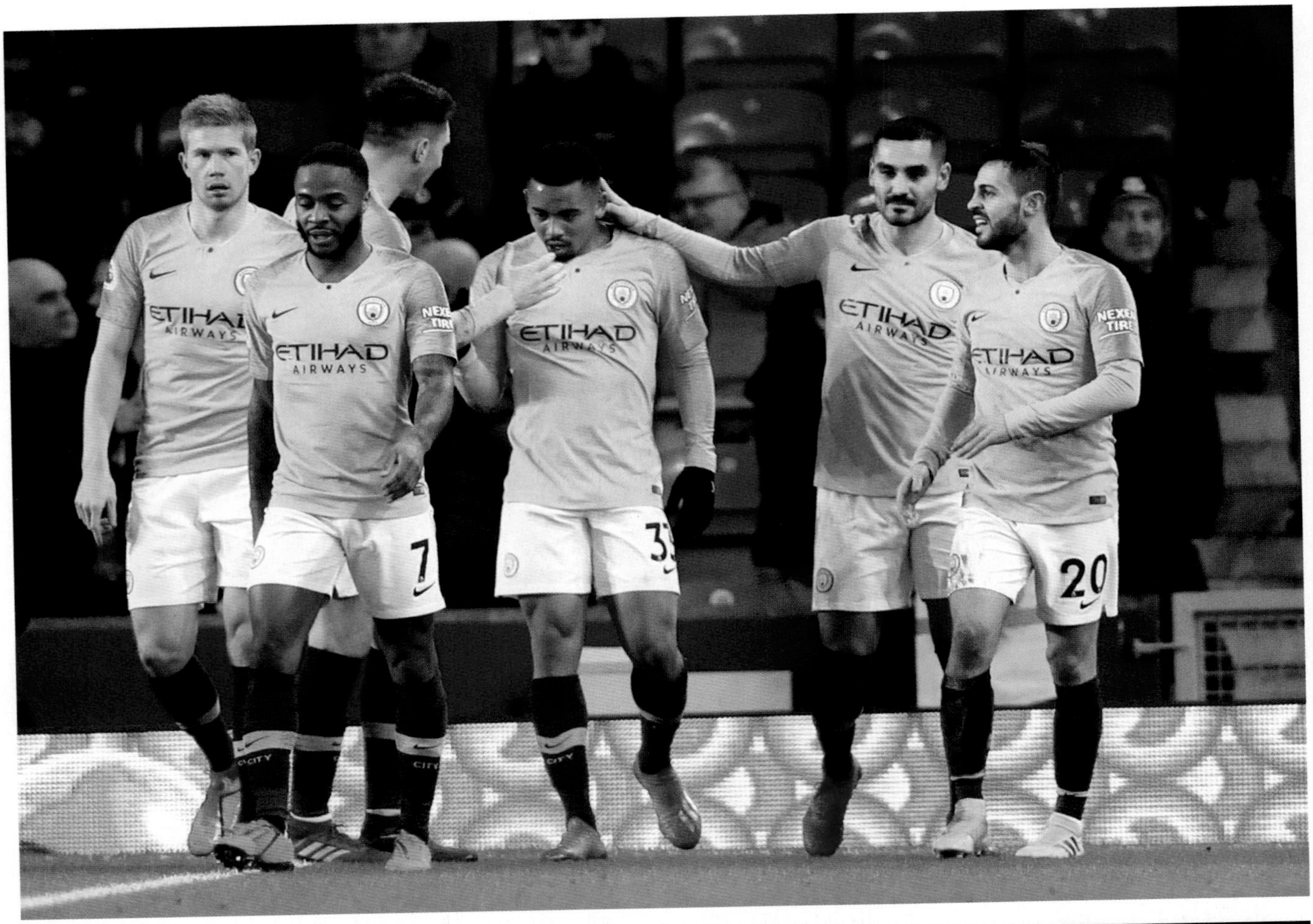
ETIHAD AIRWAYS
20

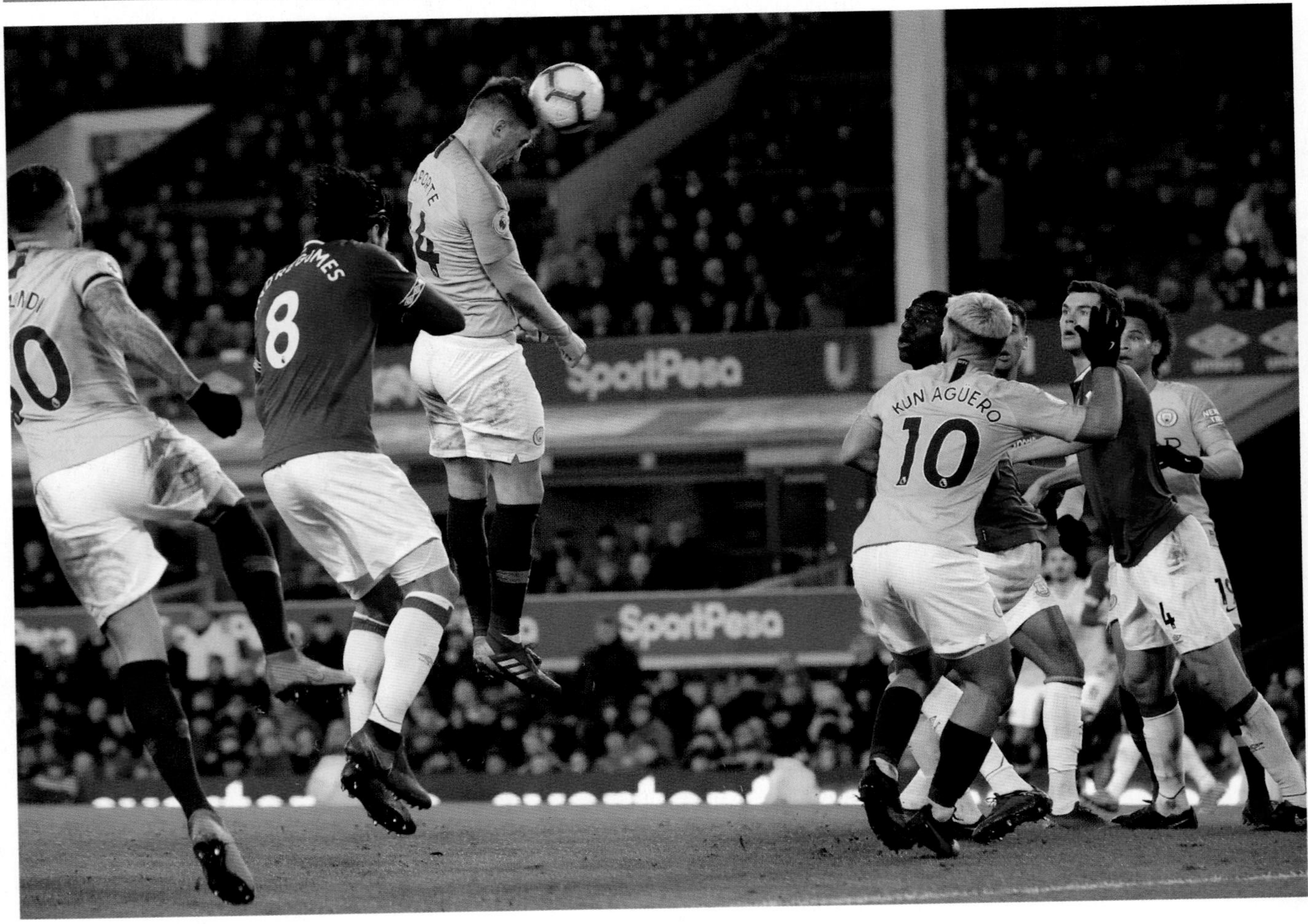
SportPesa
KUN AGUERO
10
8

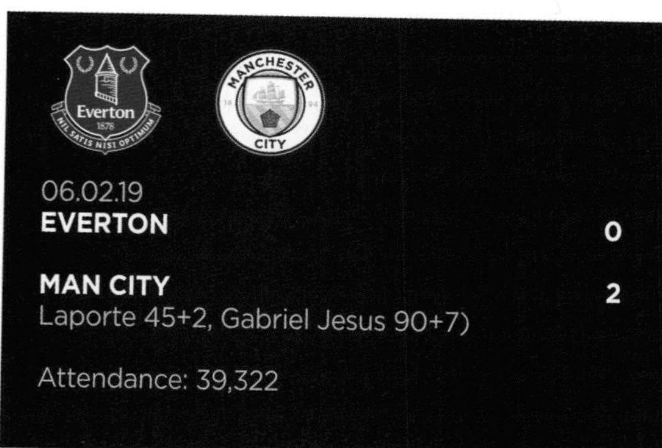

Everton
06.02.19
EVERTON 0
MAN CITY 2
Laporte 45+2, Gabriel Jesus 90+7)
Attendance: 39,322

'WE ARE IN A SITUATION WHERE WE COULD HAVE GIVEN UP BUT IT DIDN'T HAPPEN. THESE PLAYERS HAVE SHOWN INCREDIBLE DESIRE AND PERFORMANCES FOR THE LAST TWO YEARS. HOW COULD I QUESTION THEM?'

poker match, it seemed Liverpool might be blinking first, as they again dropped points the night after with a 1-1 draw with West Ham United.

The gap was now down to just one win, with Spurs, who kept winning with regularity, still very much in the hunt just a couple of points behind the Blues.

Liverpool fans were suddenly hoping neighbours Everton could take points off City at Goodison Park in a quick re-match with the Toffees, but the Blues won 2-0, clinically scoring goals in first and second-half injury time through Aymeric Laporte and Gabriel Jesus to return to the top of the table for the first time in two months.

The Reds responded with a

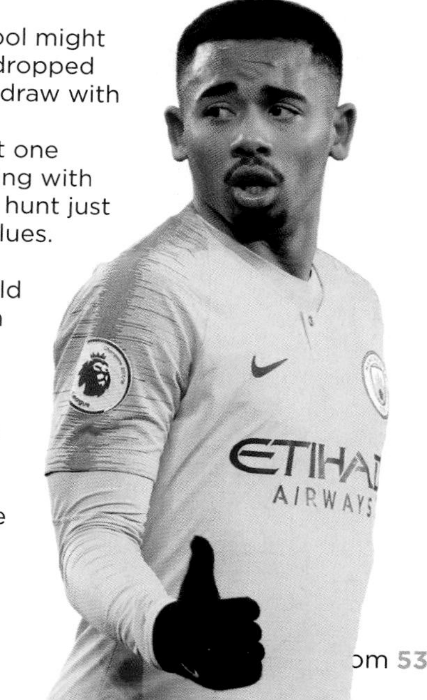

3-0 win over Bournemouth three days later to resume pole position, and there must have been hope on Merseyside that Chelsea could cause City problems again the day after. However, the Blues were ruthless from start to finish in one of the performances of the season as they thrashed Maurizio Sarri's men 6-0 with another Aguero treble, two from Raheem Sterling and another from Ilkay Gundogan seeing Pep's men go top once again – though Liverpool had one game in hand, away to Manchester United.

Afterwards, Pep said: "To score six against Chelsea and the way we played, we had so much attention. We did it, it's an incredible compliment to the players, they are outstanding. We spoke this morning, we trained set pieces, trained some movements and I never thought we would score this amount of goals."

10.02.19
MAN CITY 6
(Sterling 4, 80, Aguero 13, 19, pen 56, Gundogan 25)
CHELSEA 0
Attendance: 54,452

The intense rivalry between United and Liverpool ensured that the Manchester Reds were never going to make life easy for Klopp's side and despite losing three players to injury before half-time, United ground out a 0-0 draw at Old

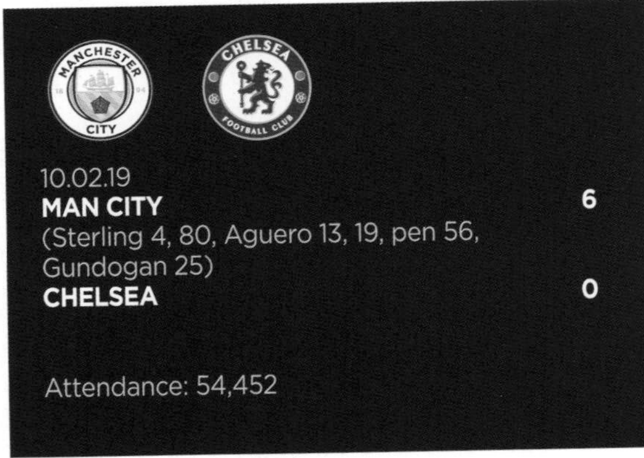

ETIHAD PLAYER OF THE MONTH

35
OLEKSANDR ZINCHENKO

FEBRUARY

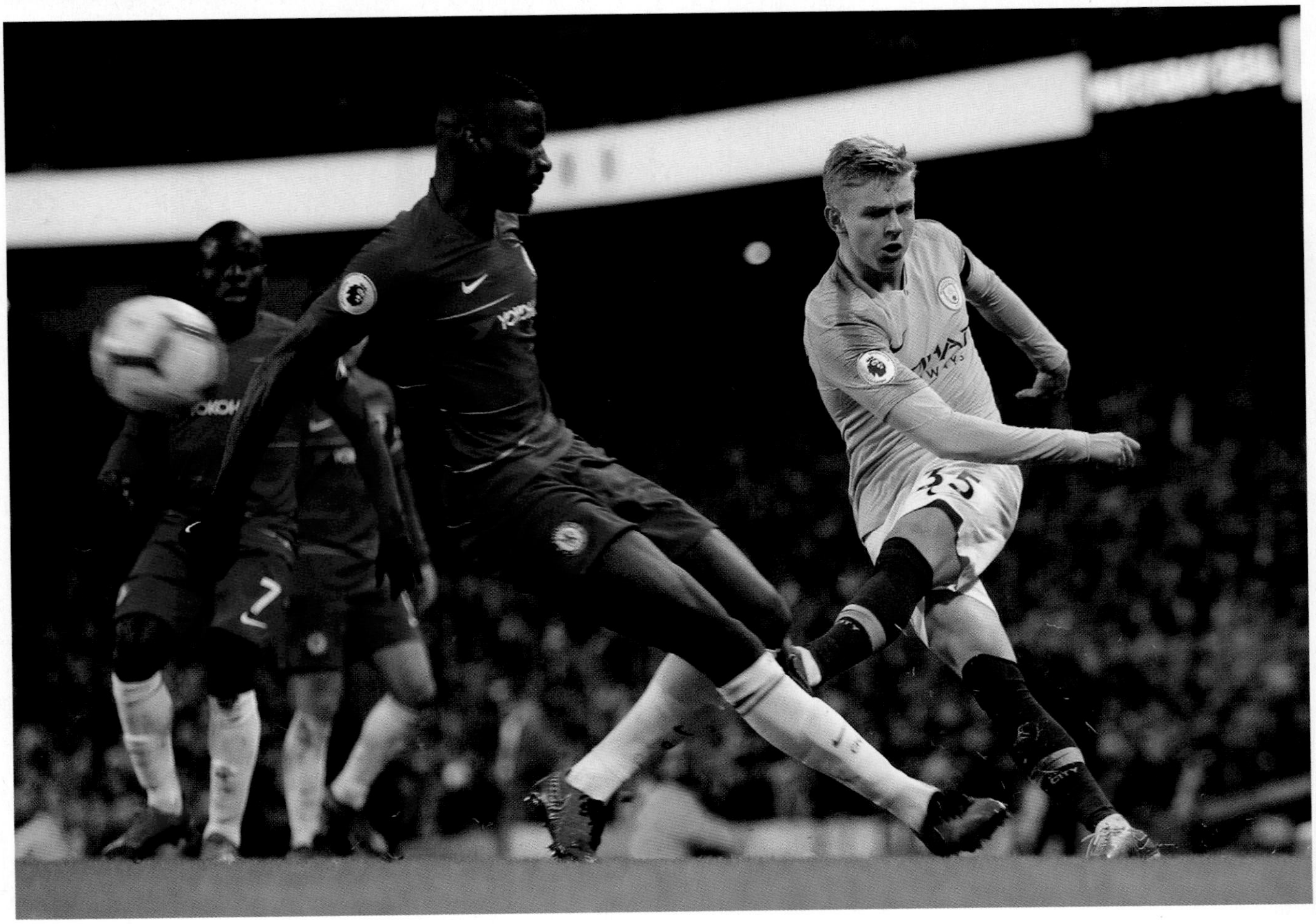

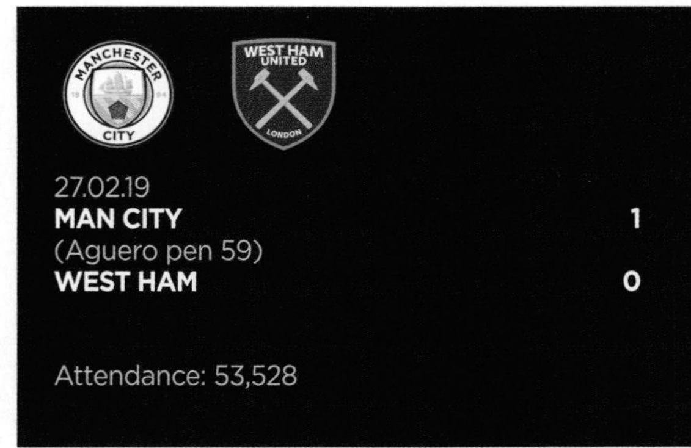

27.02.19
MAN CITY 1
(Aguero pen 59)
WEST HAM 0
Attendance: 53,528

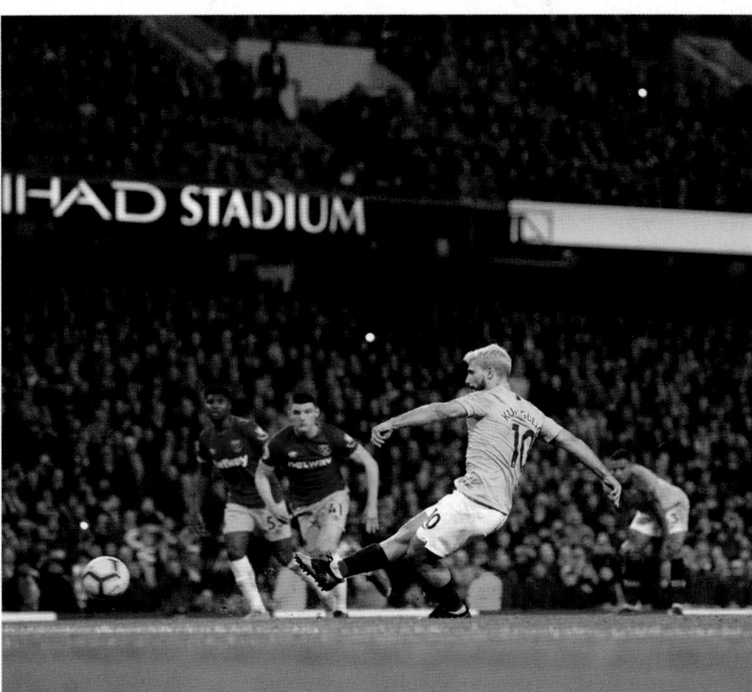

FEBRUARY

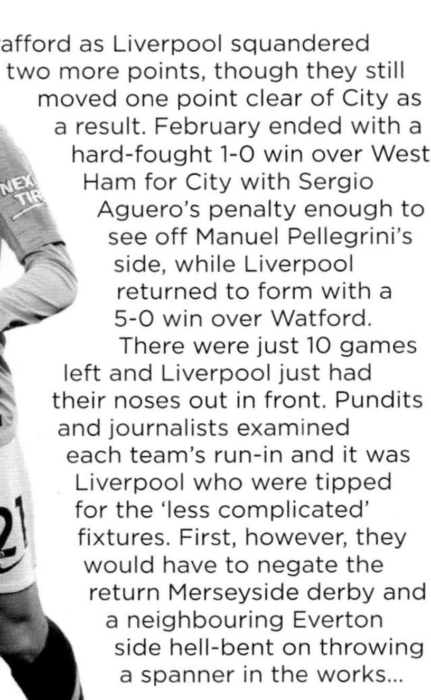

Trafford as Liverpool squandered two more points, though they still moved one point clear of City as a result. February ended with a hard-fought 1-0 win over West Ham for City with Sergio Aguero's penalty enough to see off Manuel Pellegrini's side, while Liverpool returned to form with a 5-0 win over Watford.

There were just 10 games left and Liverpool just had their noses out in front. Pundits and journalists examined each team's run-in and it was Liverpool who were tipped for the 'less complicated' fixtures. First, however, they would have to negate the return Merseyside derby and a neighbouring Everton side hell-bent on throwing a spanner in the works...

BACK AT THE TOP

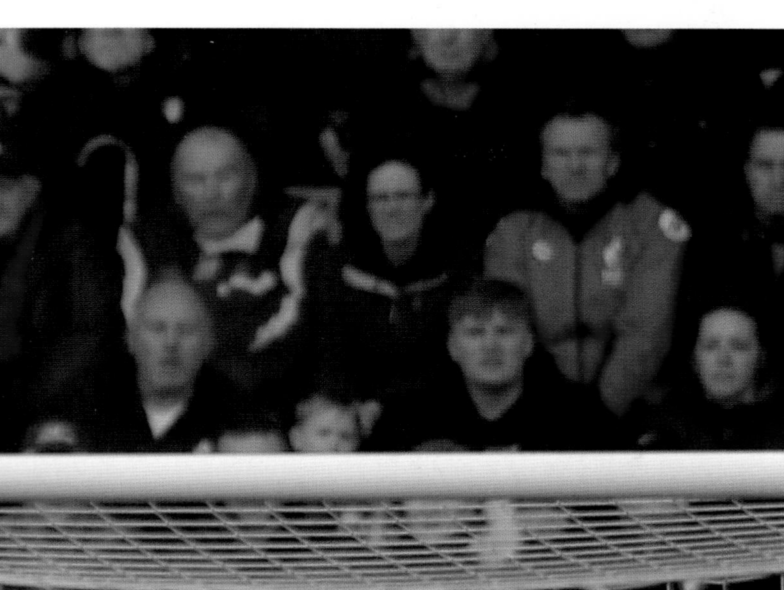

02.03.19

BOURNEMOUTH 0

MAN CITY 1
(Mahrez 55)

Attendance: 10,699

TV scheduling meant that, in the weeks that remained of the 2018/19 campaign, City and Liverpool would rarely start on the same day at the same time. As a result, the Blues kicked off March with a trip to Bournemouth and it was perhaps the first time we saw a slight shift in an already steely mentality by the defending champions.

There was a more cautious approach the game at The Vitality with the knowledge that so much hard work had gone into chipping away at Liverpool's lead that the pressure had to be kept firmly on the leaders. One poor performance

‘WE DEMAND A LOT OF THE PLAYERS WITHOUT GIVING THEM THE TIME TO REST PHYSIOLOGICALLY, THAT IS WHY IT IS INCREDIBLE. NO MATTER WHAT HAPPENS THIS SEASON THEY DESERVE MY ADMIRATION’

could prove decisive on the run-in, so while Riyad Mahrez’s second-half strike was enough to secure a hard-fought 1-0 win, it was only the three points that mattered, not so much the style in which victory was achieved.

Just 24 hours later, Everton hosted Liverpool at Goodison Park and if this was a game where the Reds feared they might drop points again, their concerns would have been well-founded as the Toffees deservedly claimed a damaging 0-0 draw. Liverpool had now dropped eight points from their past six games and City were finally back on top.

The following weekend, the Blues again played

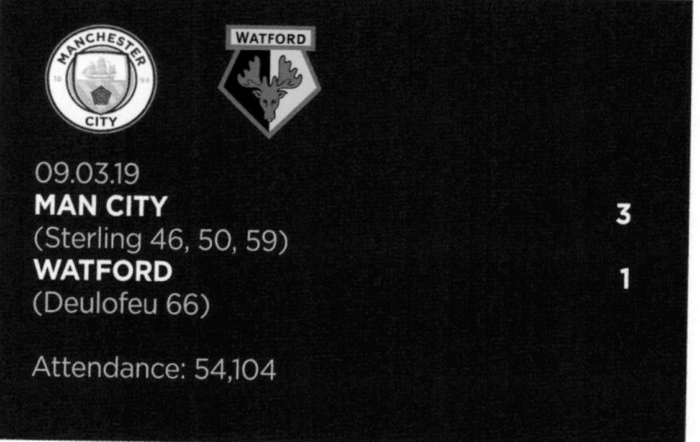

09.03.19

MAN CITY 3

(Sterling 46, 50, 59)

WATFORD 1

(Deulofeu 66)

Attendance: 54,104

first and Raheem Sterling's 13-minute hat-trick was enough to see off a stubborn Watford 3-1 at the Etihad, while Liverpool saw off Burnley 4-2 at Anfield the following day.

City's FA Cup involvement meant re-arranging several fixtures and also gave Liverpool the chance to regain top spot with a trip to struggling Fulham. When the Cottagers levelled late in the game, it seemed a gift from the gods from the Blues, especially if the West London side could hold on – but a controversial late penalty from James Milner saw the Reds secure a narrow 2-1 win at Craven Cottage. Liverpool's habit of grabbing late winners was annoyingly

'THE FIRST 15-20 MINUTES WAS INCREDIBLE WITH THE WAY WE PLAYED. AFTER THE INTERNATIONAL BREAK YOU USUALLY MISS A BIT WITH YOUR RHYTHM, BUT THE EFFORT WAS THERE'

30.03.19
FULHAM 0

MAN CITY 2
(Bernardo 5, Aguero 27)

Attendance: 25,001

SERGIO RICO
25

impressive! And it was to Fulham that City next headed to at the end of March with a comfortable 2-0 win in glorious Craven Cottage sunshine sending the Blues back to the top of the table, ahead of Liverpool's game the following day where yet another late winner kept the Merseysiders firmly on track, though City supporters must have watched on in dismay as Tottenham first squandered a great chance to win the game before conceding a comical own goal on 90 minutes.

So, going into April, Liverpool remained top by two points but had played one game more. There was no margin for error for either side with both teams now firmly focused on the finish line...

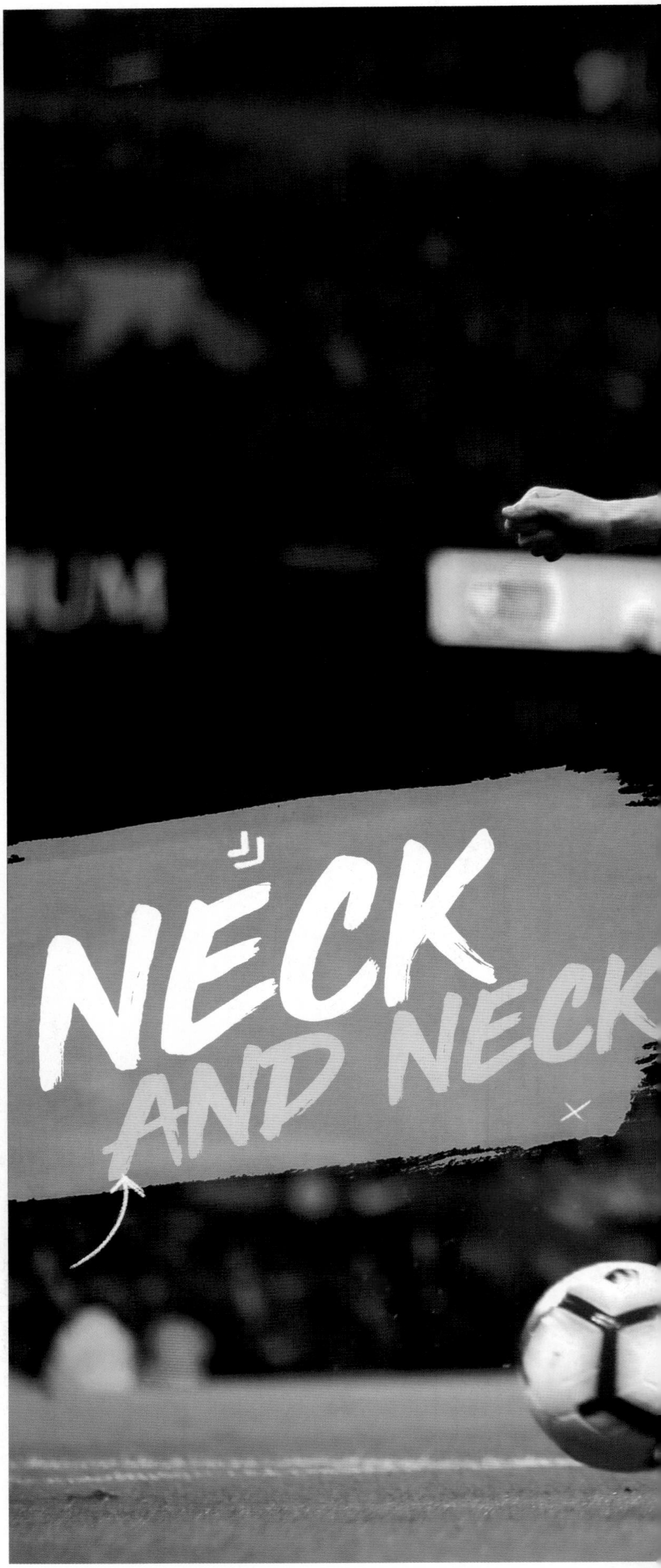

NECK AND NECK

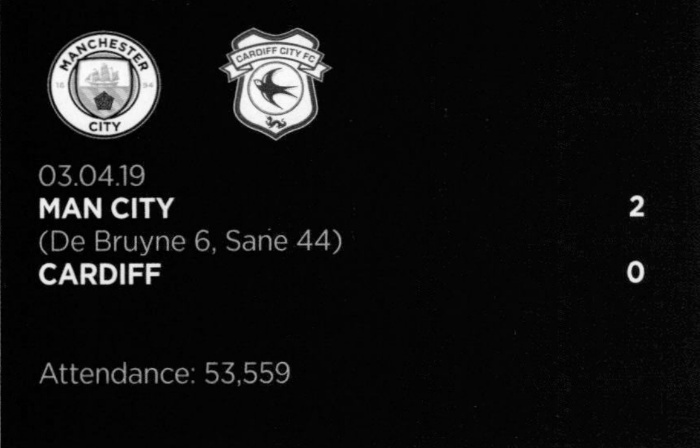

City's continuing FA Cup progress meant the home clash with Cardiff was brought forward from its original date and goals from Kevin De Bruyne and Leroy Sane were enough to secure a 2-0 win over Neil Warnock's side and put the Blues top again.

Liverpool responded with a 3-1 win at Southampton having initially been behind and then still level after 80 minutes before scoring twice late on. It was the third game in a row where things could easily have gone wrong for the Merseysiders – but didn't.

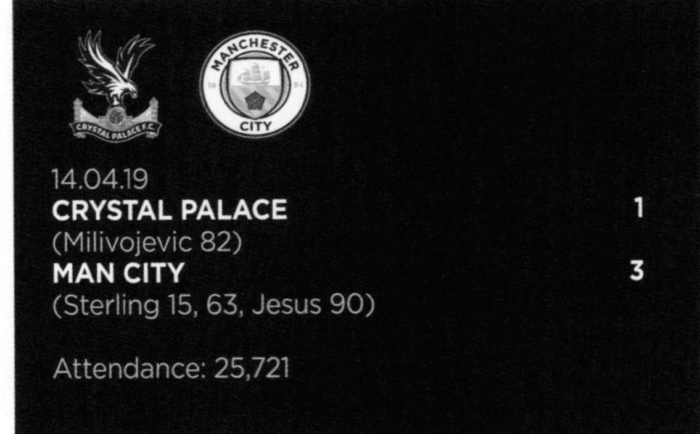

14.04.19
CRYSTAL PALACE 1
(Milivojevic 82)
MAN CITY 3
(Sterling 15, 63, Jesus 90)

Attendance: 25,721

Next up, both teams would play consecutively on Sunday 14 April. City travelled to Crystal Palace who had inflicted a damaging defeat at the Etihad back in December while Liverpool hosted Chelsea. Each set of fans had hope the other would come unstuck and the Blues knew Selhurst Park would be a genuine test given the first meeting between the clubs. City, however, took the game by the scruff of the neck and came out determined and focused, never allowing the hosts to get going and, apart from a late scare, City won 3-1 to again go top of the table. Liverpool responded with an unfussy 2-0 win over Chelsea to maintain pole position.

There were other factors to consider in the weeks that remained, too. City's next game was against Tottenham – the side who had just eliminated the Blues from the Champions League during an exhausting second leg at the Etihad. Three games in 11 days against a Spurs team who sat third in the Premier League was a big ask and City had to dig deep to grind out a 1-0 win courtesy of Phil Foden's header and a raucous Etihad crowd. It felt like a huge three points for the Blues, particularly as Liverpool were away to Cardiff the following day – a game they were expected to win – and, of course, did.

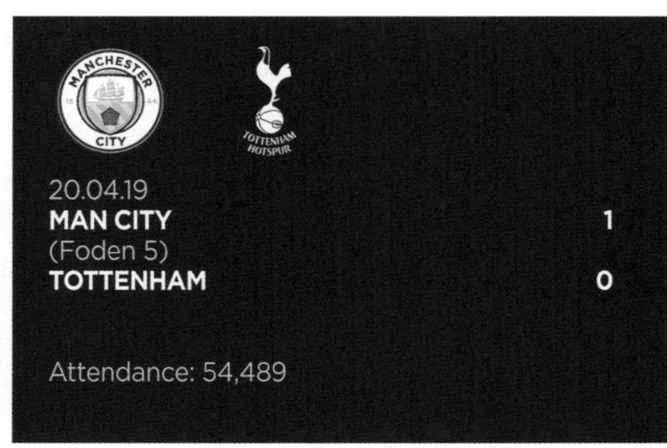

20.04.19
MAN CITY 1
(Foden 5)
TOTTENHAM 0

Attendance: 54,489

24.04.19
MAN UTD 0

MAN CITY 2
(Bernardo 55, Sane 66)

Attendance: 74,431

Perhaps the key to the title race was whether City could win the game in hand over Liverpool and the fact it was against Manchester United at Old Trafford had Liverpool fans licking their lips that this could finally be where the destiny swung back in their favour. United, fresh from a 4-0 thrashing at Everton, had been heavily criticised by their fans and the media with manager Ole Gunnar Solskjaer promising there would be a reaction against City, and as the teams went off 0-0 at the break at Old Trafford, it had been a far from convincing display by the Blues.

But City re-emerged looking much more their old selves and goals from Bernardo and Leroy Sane midway through the second period gave Pep's men a priceless 2-0 win over the Reds, though there was still plenty of hard work ahead. Liverpool ended April with an easy 5-0 win over relegated Huddersfield Town while City had to travel to face freshly-safe from relegation Burnley at Turf Moor.

ETIHAD
AIRWAYS
20

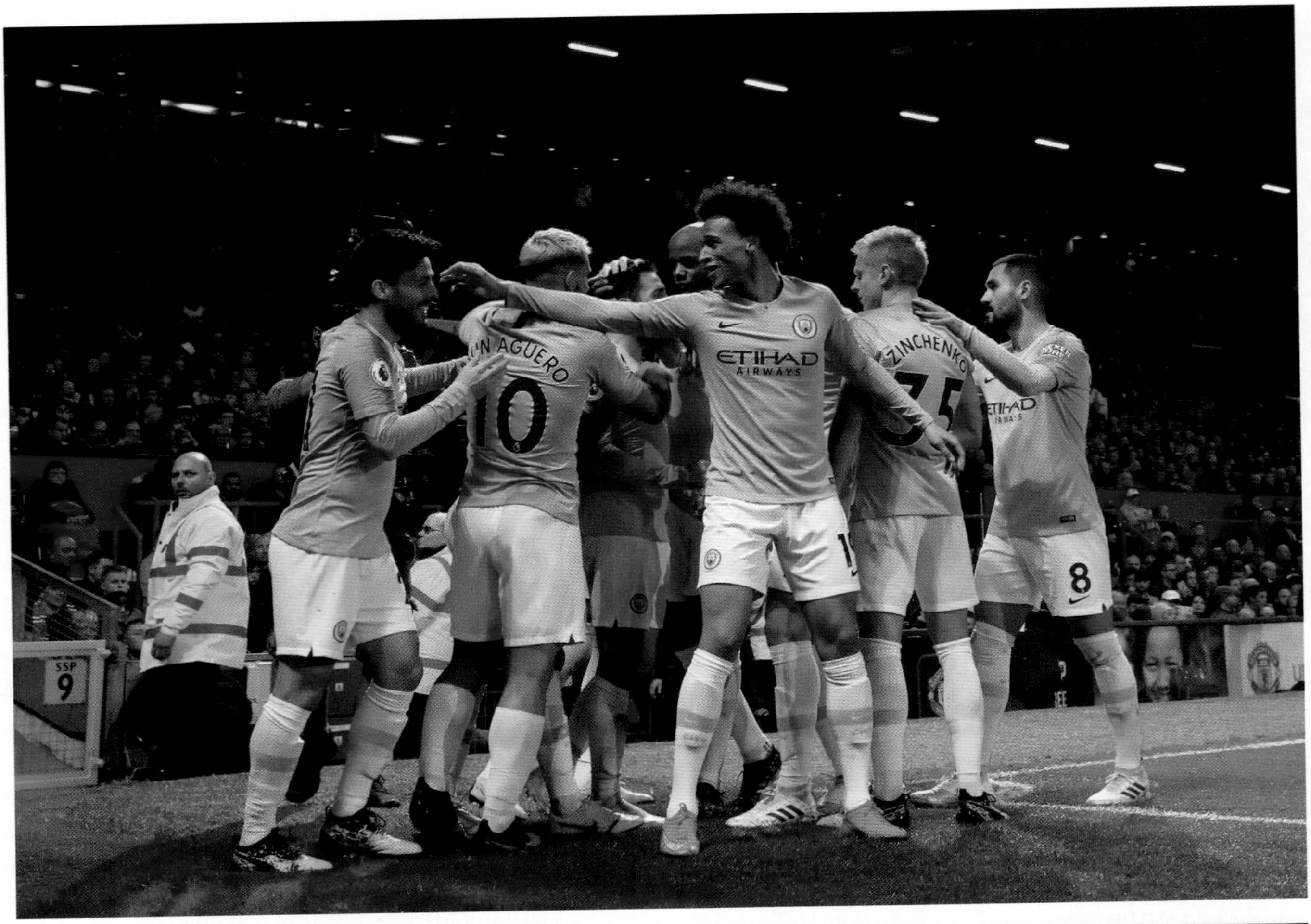
AGUERO
10
ETIHAD
AIRWAYS
ZINCHENKO
8
SSP
9

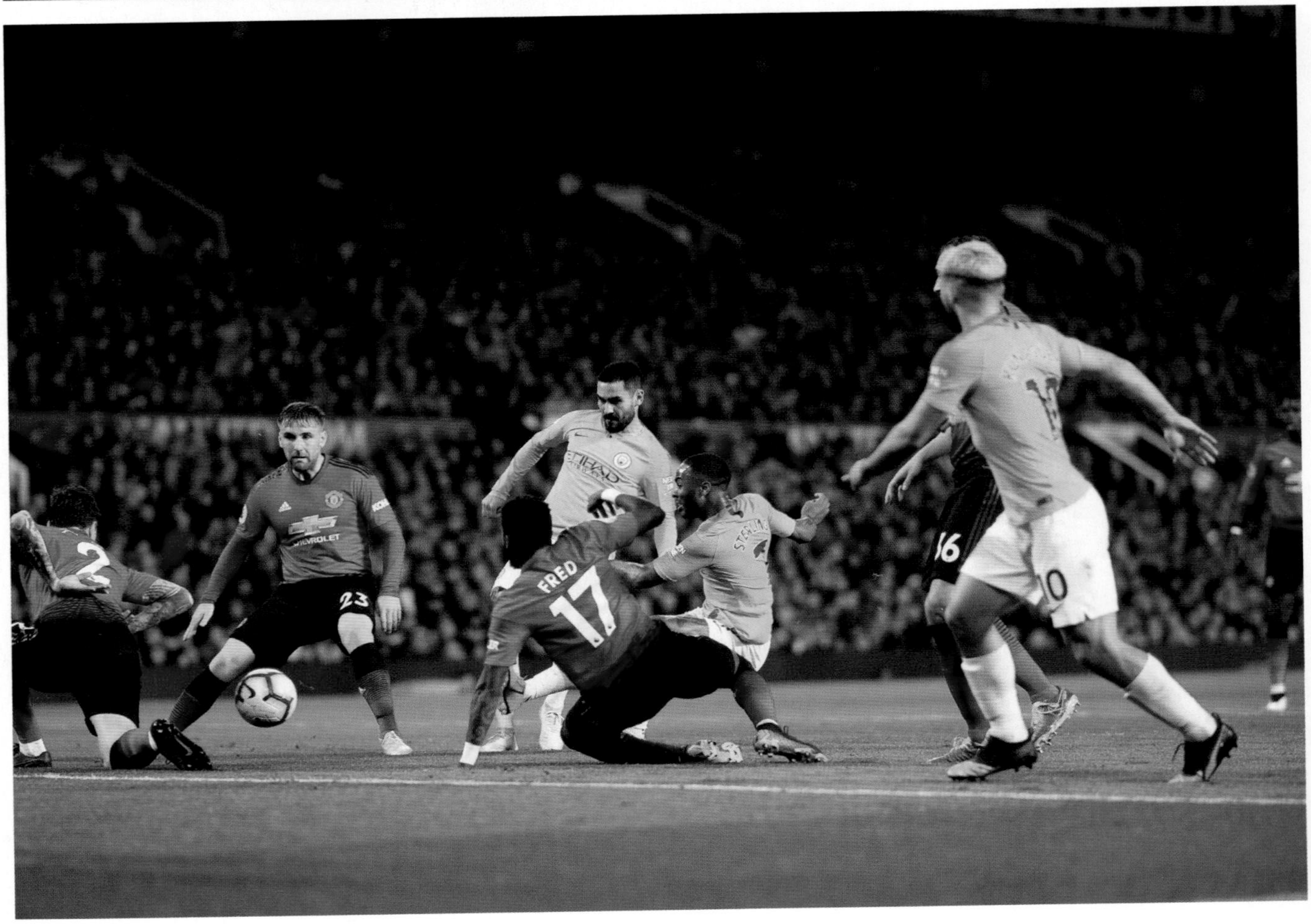
FRED
17
23

APRIL

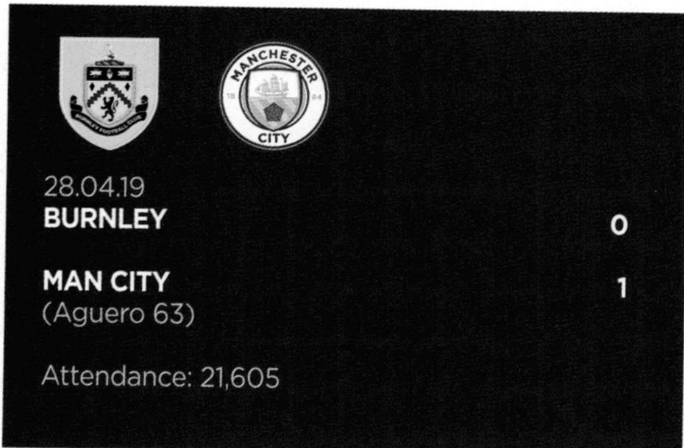

28.04.19
BURNLEY 0

MAN CITY 1
(Aguero 63)

Attendance: 21,605

The Clarets were up for the scrap, as expected, and frustrated the Blues until the 63rd minute when Sergio Aguero's shot was seemingly scrambled off the line – only for technology to signal the ball had crossed the line by a couple of millimetres. Fine margins indeed.

That was enough for City to win 1-0. Two games remained for Pep's side – and two wins would guarantee back-to-back titles.

GLORIOUS FINALE

06.05.19
MAN CITY 1
(Kompany 70)
LEICESTER 0

Attendance: 54,506

Liverpool's penultimate game of the Premier League season was away to Newcastle United, managed by former Reds' boss Rafa Benitez. Journalists and pundits pondered if there would be one final twist in this enthralling title race. Could Benitez, adored by Liverpool fans, be the man to end their 29-year wait for the top-flight title? For a time, it seemed he might. Newcastle, roared on by a buoyant St James' Park crowd, exchanged blows with the Reds and with just five minutes left, the score was 2-2 – but when Fabinho won a free-kick on the right of the Magpies' box, there felt an air of inevitability as Divock Origi glanced home what was certain to be the winning goal.

Had that not gone in, City could have gone into the final home game of the season knowing that, in all likelihood, one win from the last two matches would be enough – instead, it was again win or bust with Liverpool two points

14

ETIHAD
2

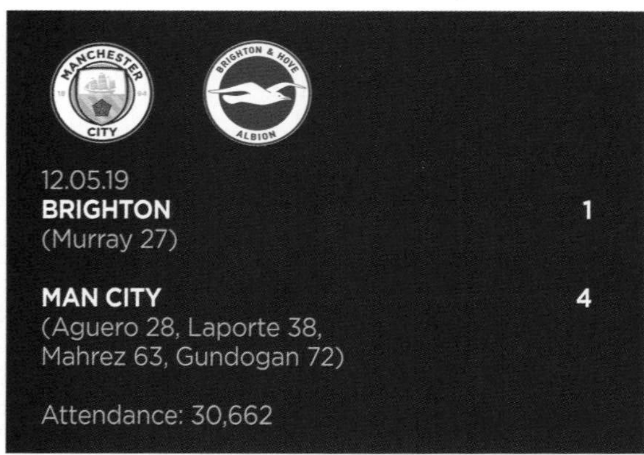

12.05.19
BRIGHTON 1
(Murray 27)

MAN CITY 4
(Aguero 28, Laporte 38, Mahrez 63, Gundogan 72)

Attendance: 30,662

clear. And the irony of having former Liverpool manager Brendan Rodgers now in charge of Leicester City – the Blues' next opponents – suggested that there would indeed be one final twist in the tale.

The Foxes looked sharp and dangerous from the word go, with City surviving a couple of scares before going in at the break with the game goalless. As time went on, so a feeling of desperation began to creep in. The tension was unbearable and there was an air of this not being City's night and that it would be Leicester who would effectively end the Blues' hopes of back-to-back titles. Then, from nowhere, a goal worthy of winning any competition. With 70 minutes played, Vincent Kompany received the ball midway inside the Foxes' half, nudged the ball forward, teed himself up and with the majority of the Etihad screaming 'don't shoot', the Belgian unleashed a swerving drive from 25 yards that rocketed into the top right-hand corner.

The Etihad went crazy. Surely Captain Fantastic wasn't going to be the hero again – just as he had been so many times during his long City career? It was fairy-tale stuff, but the game wasn't over. In the dying minutes, Leicester broke forward with purpose and when the ball fell to former City striker Kelechi Iheanacho, the Foxes sub swept a low shot well wide when he looked odds-on to score. Not long after, the whistle blew for full-time. City were just 90 minutes away from being crowned champions once again.

An absorbing title race, where the leadership had changed an incredible 32 times during the course of the campaign, was just 90 minutes from its conclusion. It had been like a 38-game penalty shoot-out, with City up last, knowing one more win would seal it.

The Blues had to travel to Brighton on the final day, while Liverpool hosted Wolves. Would there, after all, be one more cruel chapter for either side?

When Sadio Mane gave the Reds a 1-0 lead on 17 minutes, Liverpool vaulted above City in the 'as it stands' live Premier League table. It seemed as though it had to happen that the drama levels were cranked to breaking point one last time. Ten minutes later and Anfield erupted again – but this time because news of a Brighton goal at the Amex Stadium. Glenn Murray had nodded the Seagulls ahead and now City suddenly needed two goals at least to win the game.

AMERICAN EXPRESS
COMMUNITY STAD
DON'T live life WITHOUT IT
BRUNO
2
8
8

League

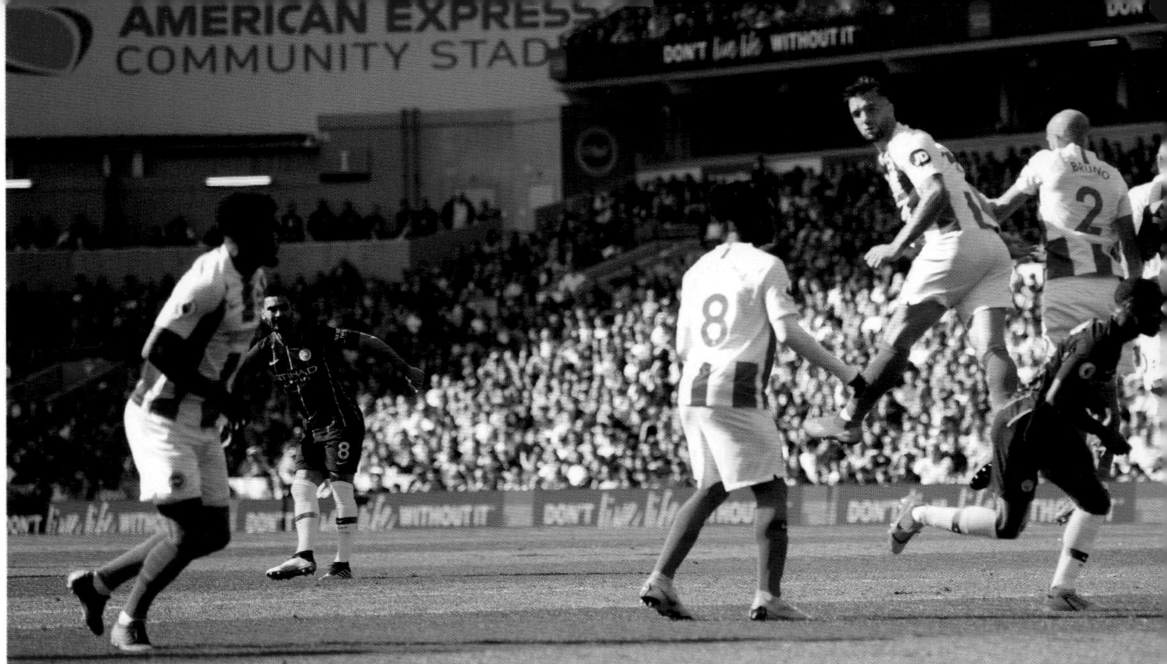

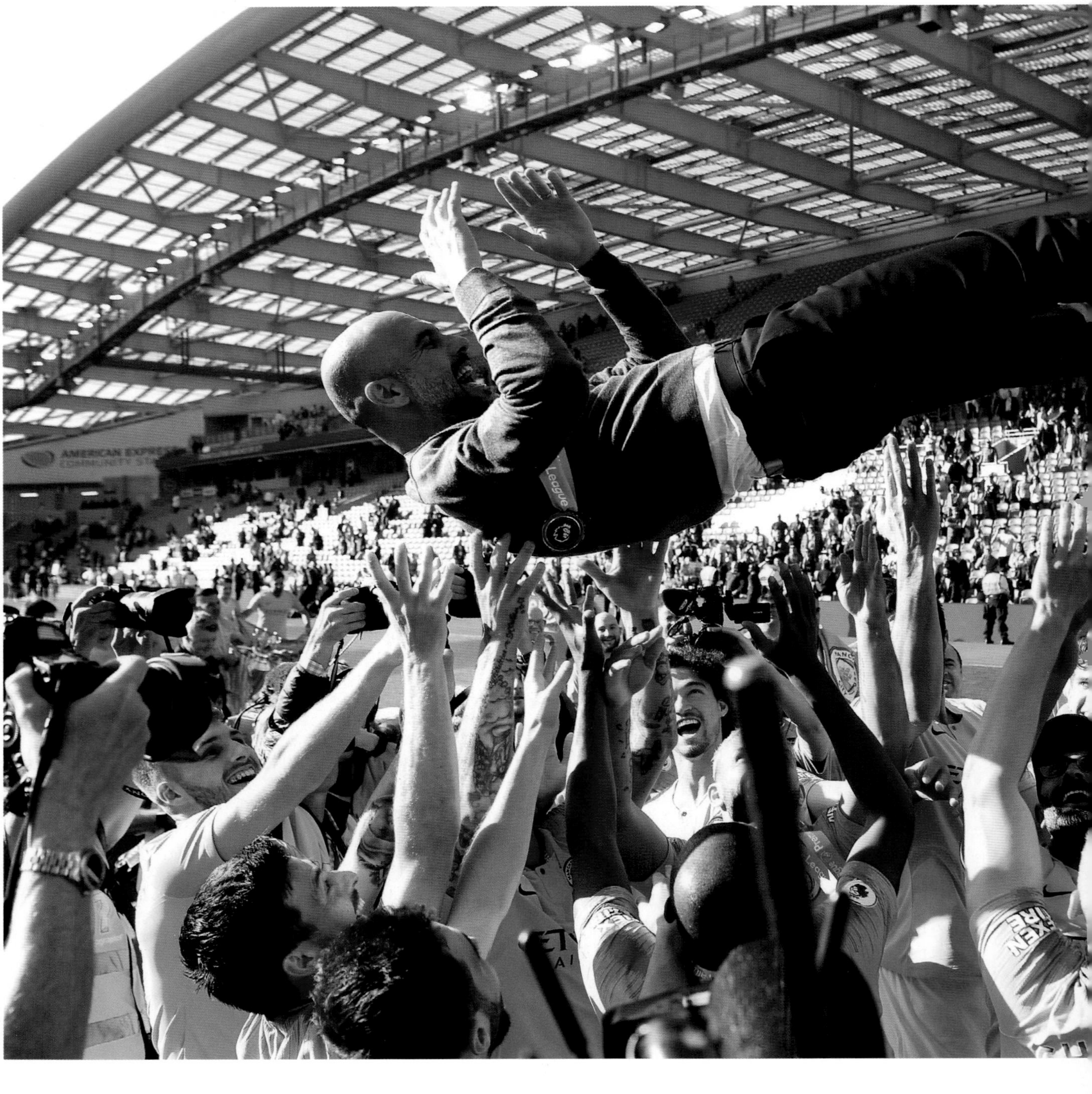

But this incredible City team, who never know when they are beaten, didn't panic or lose their cool. Anything but, in fact. Just 83 seconds after falling behind, Sergio Aguero latched on to David Silva's back-flick to score his 32nd of another prolific season. Ten minutes after that, Aymeric Laporte powered home Riyad Mahrez's corner and City were again leading the Premier League (as things stood).

This time, they would stay on top. It was proving to be a breathless finale and one this fantastic battle between Manchester and Merseyside demanded. Mahrez and Ilkay Gundogan both scored superb long-range efforts to seal the points after the break and though Liverpool ended with a 2-0 win over Wolves, the Blues' 4-1 win at Brighton meant Jurgen Klopp's side had finally run out of games and City were champions. The Blues had won their last 14 Premier League games in succession and finished with 98 points – just as Pep had predicted they would have to do and were just two points shy of the 100 total from 2017/18. Liverpool finished on 97 – the highest runner-up total ever and, in any other season prior to 2017, enough to win the title.

However, for all their efforts, it was the sky blue and white ribbons that blew gently in the warm Sussex breeze at the Amex Stadium. City were champions and perhaps the greatest title race of all time was over.

2018/19 CARABAO CUP WINNERS

THIRD ROUND
25.09.18
OXFORD 0
MAN CITY 3
GOALS:
Jesus 36, Mahrez 78,
Foden 90+2
Attendance: 11,956

Pep Guardiola's team selection from the first game to the last underlined his intention to win the Carabao Cup for a second successive season.

City's quest for the trophy that has had many sponsorships over the years, but is best known as the League Cup, began with an away trip to League One strugglers Oxford United. The U's

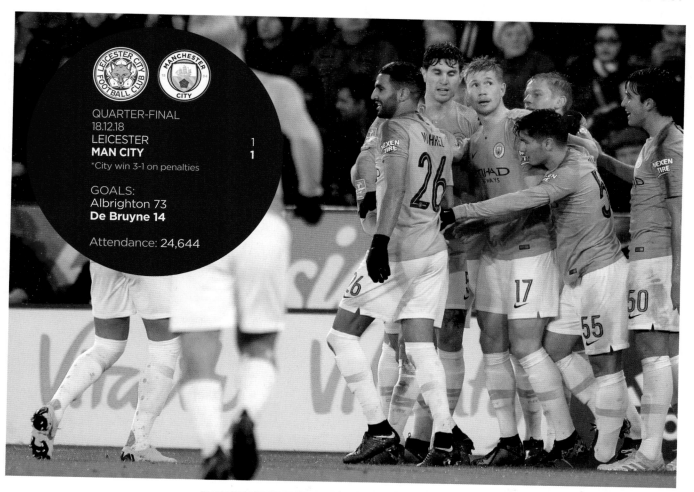

QUARTER-FINAL
18.12.18

LEICESTER	1
MAN CITY	**1**

*City win 3-1 on penalties

GOALS:
Albrighton 73
De Bruyne 14

Attendance: 24,644

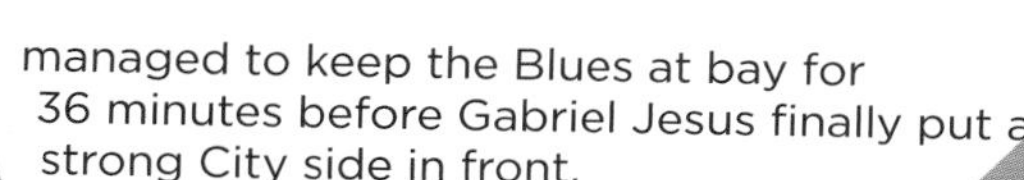

managed to keep the Blues at bay for 36 minutes before Gabriel Jesus finally put a strong City side in front.

Further goals after the break from Riyad Mahrez and Phil Foden completed a comfortable 3-0 victory and a passage into the next round.

City faced Premier League rivals Fulham at the Etihad in the fourth round and though the Cottagers put on a decent show, two goals from youngster Brahim Diaz secured a 2-0 victory and a quarter-final spot with Leicester City.

The clash with the Foxes proved to be a difficult evening for the Carabao Cup holders and though Kevin De Bruyne fired City ahead, Leicester

SEMI-FINAL FIRST LEG
09.01.19

MAN CITY	**9**
BURTON ALBION	0

GOALS:
De Bruyne 6, Jesus 30, 34, 57, 65, Zinchenko 37, Foden 62, Walker 70, Mahrez 83

Attendance: 32,089

levelled and took the game into extra time and, eventually penalties. During the shoot-out, City keeper Aro Muric saved two penalties and as City won 3-1 to move into the semi-finals and a two-legged tie with Burton Albion.

The first leg saw the Blues run riot, seeing off Nigel Clough's side 9-0 at the Etihad with Gabriel Jesus grabbing four of the goals where City showed their ruthlessness from beginning to end. The result rendered the second leg a formality, with Sergio Aguero grabbing the only goal of the game to complete a 10-0 aggregate victory.

The Carabao Cup final at Wembley saw City and

SEMI-FINAL SECOND LEG
23.01.19

BURTON ALBION	0
MAN CITY	**1**

GOALS:
Aguero 26

Attendance: 6,519

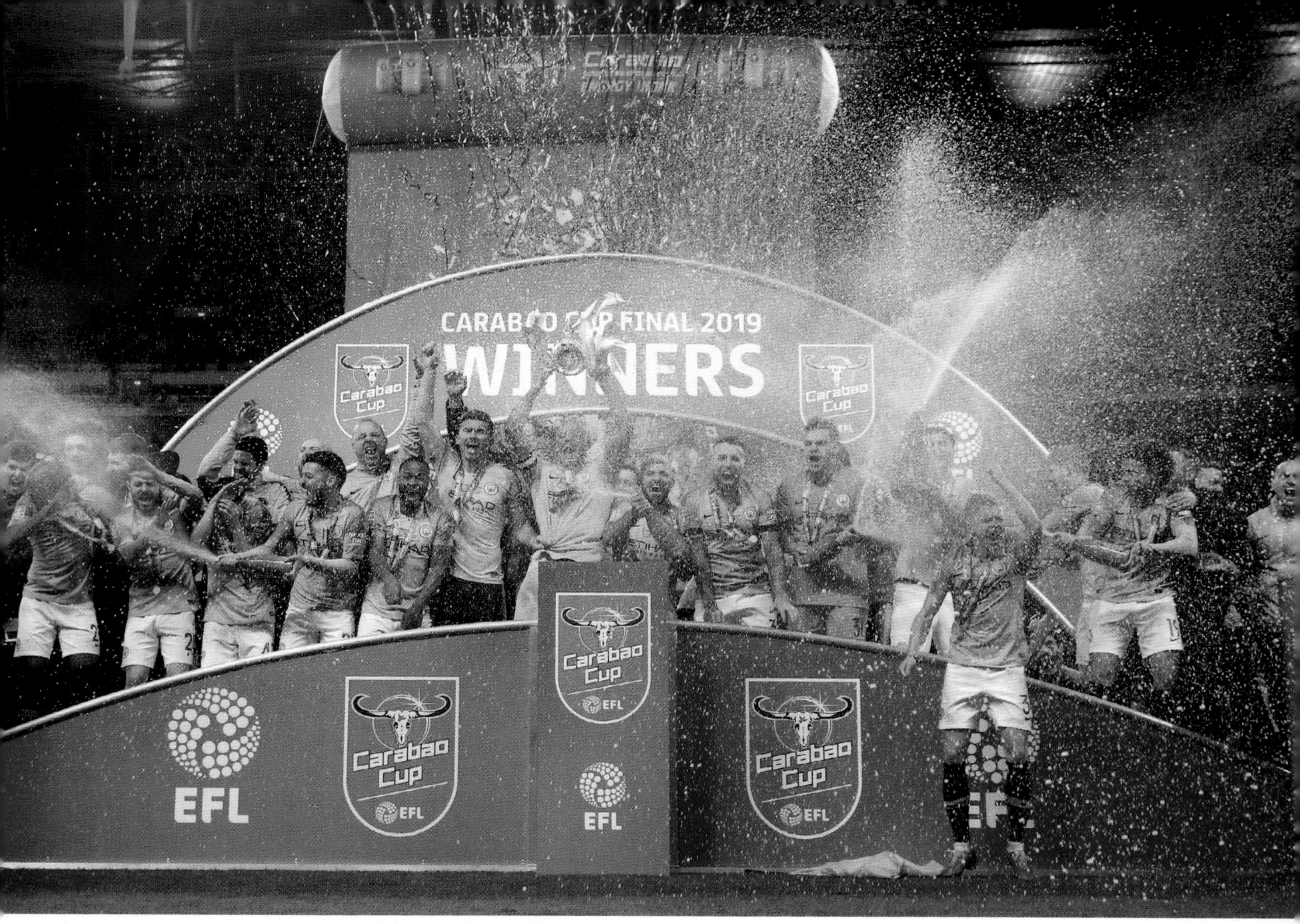

Chelsea compete for the trophy in a tight, tense battle that saw neither side find the net in 90 minutes or the ensuing extra time during which Chelsea looked the more likely to go and win the game. Yet again the Blues were going to have to win the trophy the hard way – on penalties.

Jorginho was first to miss, with Leroy Sane missing for City with the score at 2-2. David Luiz then striking the post straight after with ultimately, Raheem Sterling emphatically settling the shoot-out 4-3 in City's favour to secure the Carabao Cup for a second successive season.

FA CUP THE JOURNEY

Without success in the FA Cup since 2011, City began their quest for the trophy with a third-round tie at home to Championship side Rotherham United.

In front of more than 52,000 fans at the Etihad, City thrashed the South Yorkshire side 7-0, with seven different players on the scoresheet. The Blues were again drawn at home to Premier League rivals Burnley in the fourth round and again, were merciless against the Clarets. More than 50,000 fans saw City triumph 5-0 to progress to the last 16 with minimum fuss.

ROUND 3 06.01.19
MAN CITY **7**
ROTHERHAM 0

GOALS:
Sterling 12, Foden 43, Ajayi o.g 45+1, Jesus 52, Mahrez 73, Otamendi 78, Sane 85

Attendance: 52,708

ROUND 4 26.01.19
MAN CITY **5**
BURNLEY 0

GOALS:
Jesus 23, B Silva 52, De Bruyne 61, Long og 73, Aguero pen 85

Attendance: 50,121

ROUND 5 16.02.19
NEWPORT COUNTY 1
MAN CITY **4**

GOALS:
Amond 88
Sane 51, Foden 75, 89, Mahrez 90

Attendance: 9,680

City were drawn against Newport County in the fifth round with a trip to Rodney Parade for the reigning Premier League champions. The Exiles proved tricky opposition on a difficult playing surface and the League 2 minnows went into the break with the score still 0-0.

The breakthrough came on 51 minutes when Leroy Sane put City ahead and though Newport held on until 75 minutes when Phil Foden doubled the visitors' lead. The Exiles pulled one back on 89 minutes, before Foden responded immediately and Riyad Mahrez completed the scoring in added time to give the Blues a 4-1 win in South Wales.

The FA Cup sixth round saw City drawn against lower league opposition for the third time in four ties, but Swansea were anything but an easy passage to the semi-finals. In fact, the Swans opened up a shock 2-0 at half-time and it wasn't until Bernardo's 69th-minute thunderbolt that City finally suggested a comeback.

When Raheem Sterling was felled in the box on 78 minutes, Sergio Aguero struck his penalty against the post and in off the goalkeeper to level the scores and, two minutes from time, Aguero headed home Bernardo's cross to seal a dramatic victory.

City were back at Wembley with Brighton the semi-final opponents and Watford faced Wolves the following day. Gabriel Jesus scored the only goal of the game just four minutes in to secure a final place for the first time since 2013 – Watford would provide the opposition for the showpiece final.

QUARTER-FINAL 16.03.19

SWANSEA	2
MAN CITY	**3**

GOALS:
Grimes pen 20, Celina 29
B Silva 69, Nordfeldt og 79, Aguero 88

Attendance: 19,783

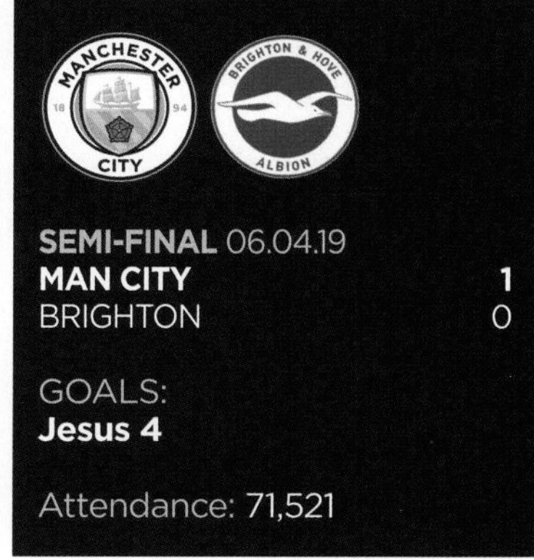

SEMI-FINAL 06.04.19

MAN CITY	**1**
BRIGHTON	0

GOALS:
Jesus 4

Attendance: 71,521

FA CUP FINAL
18.05.19

MANCHESTER CITY	**6**
WATFORD	0

GOALS:
Silva 26, Jesus 38, 68, De Bruyne 61, Sterling 81, 87

Attendance: 85,854

The FA Cup final against Watford completed the greatest season in City's history, though it was the Hornets who should have drawn first blood when Roberto Pereyra raced through on 11 minutes only to be denied by a fine Ederson save.

The Blues survived another goalmouth scramble before steadily taking control and finally taking the lead when Raheem Sterling's header fell to David Silva, who hit a low shot past Hercules Gomes to put City ahead on 26 minutes.

City doubled the lead on 38 minutes when Bernardo's deep cross found Gabriel Jesus, who angled a volley past Gomes.

After the break, City were rampant and when Jesus broke free in the Watford half, the Brazilian unselfishly passed to Kevin De Bruyne, who sent the keeper the wrong way before slotting home the third just past the hour.

Seven minutes later, Jesus doubled his personal tally when he again raced clear to seal the game with only 68 minutes on the clock. But City were far from finished.

On 81 minutes, Bernardo drove into the Watford box before whipping a low drive in that Sterling finished from close range, and the England winger completed the rout on 87 minutes.

It was the perfect way to end an incredible season as the Blues became the first men's English side to win all four domestic trophies. Fourmidable indeed!

2018/19 CHAMPIONS LEAGUE

02.10.18
TSG HOFFENHEIM 1
(Belfodil 1)
MAN CITY 2
(Aguero 8, D Silva 87)

Attendance: 24,851

19.09.18
MAN CITY 1
(D Silva 67)
LYON 2
(Cornet 26, Fekir 43)

Attendance: 40,111

City's 2018/19 Champions League was thrilling, nail-biting and ultimately heart-breaking.

It began with a group stage that included Lyon, Hoffenheim and Shakhtar Donetsk - a group that many expected the Blues to progress from, but the opening game against Lyon proved to be something of a shock, with the French side impressive in their 2-1 win at the Etihad.

It meant there was work to do for Pep Guardiola's side with an immediate response needed away to Hoffenheim. The game couldn't have started any worse, with the Bundesliga side ahead inside the first minute - but goals from Sergio Aguero and a David Siva winner three minutes from the end gave the Blues a priceless 2-1 win.

Shakhtar were then dispatched 3-0 in Ukraine with David Siva, Aymeric Laporte and Bernardo all on target. The return match against Shakhtar a fortnight later saw City record a record Champions League win - 6-0 at the Etihad - courtesy of a Gabriel Jesus hat-trick and further goals from David Silva, Raheem Sterling and Riyad Mahrez.

Lyon again proved stubborn opposition and only a late Aguero goal earned City a dramatic 2-2 draw. City completed the group stage with two Leroy Sane strikes securing a 2-1 win over Hoffenheim.

The Blues again faced German opposition in the Round of 16, with Schalke the obstacle for Pep Guardiola's side and a place in the quarter-finals. The first leg was a thrilling affair, with Schalke scoring two penalties just before the break to cancel out Aguero's 18th-minute goal.

City fought back - despite losing Nicolas Otamendi to a red card - and goals from Sane and Sterling securing a 3-2 victory. The second

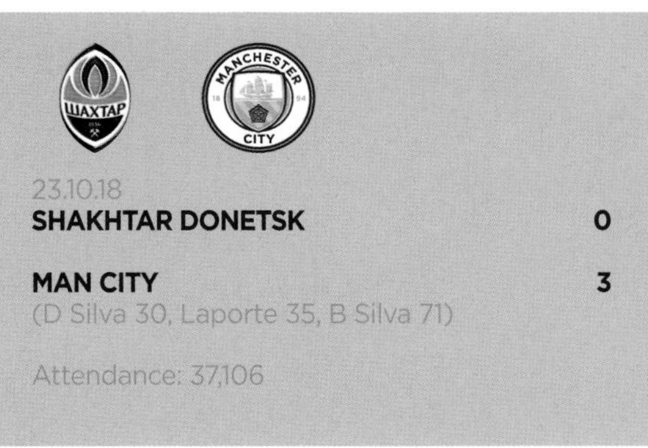

23.10.18

SHAKHTAR DONETSK **0**

MAN CITY **3**
(D Silva 30, Laporte 35, B Silva 71)

Attendance: 37,106

07.11.18

MAN CITY **6**
(D Silva 11, Jesus 24, 72, 90+2, Sterling 49, Mahrez 84)

SHAKHTAR DONETSK **0**

Attendance: 52,286

27.11.18

LYON **2**
(Cornet 55, 81)

MAN CITY **2**
(Laporte 62, Aguero 83)

Attendance: 56,039

12.12.18

MAN CITY **2**

(Sane 45+1, 61)

TSG HOFFENHEIM **1**

(Kramaric 16)

Attendance: 50,411

leg was far more comfortable as Schalke were thrashed 7-0 at the Etihad with Gabriel Jesus' hat-trick ensuing a last eight spot for Pep's men for a second year in succession.

The draw saw City pitted against fellow Premier League side Tottenham Hotspur and the first leg at the impressive new Tottenham Hotspur Stadium looked set to go City's way when a controversial penalty was awarded early in the game – but Aguero's spot-kick was saved and Spurs went on to win 1-0.

The second leg proved an unforgettable clash that swung this way, then that. In a breathless start, Sterling put City ahead after just four minutes before Son Heung-Min scored twice in four minutes to give Tottenham a huge advantage with just 10 minutes on the clock. Bernardo levelled immediately and Sterling's second not long after meant that five goals had been scored in just 21 minutes.

Aguero put City further ahead just before the hour mark to make it 4-2 on the night and put

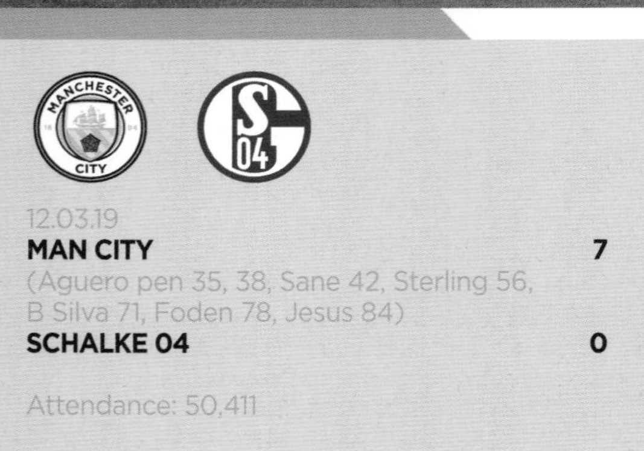

12.03.19

MAN CITY **7**

(Aguero pen 35, 38, Sane 42, Sterling 56, B Silva 71, Foden 78, Jesus 84)

SCHALKE 04 **0**

Attendance: 50,411

20.02.19

SCHALKE 04 **2**

(Bentaleb pen 38, pen 45)

MAN CITY **3**

(Aguero 18, Sane 85, Sterling 90)

Attendance: 54,417

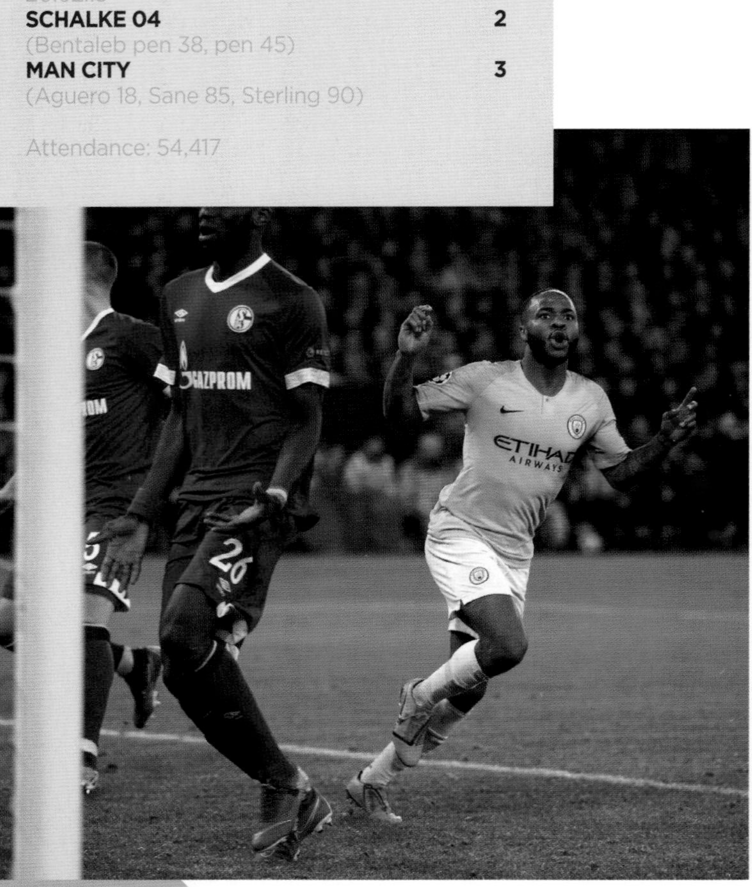

09.04.19

TOTTENHAM HOTSPUR 1
(Son 78)
MAN CITY 0

Attendance: 60,044

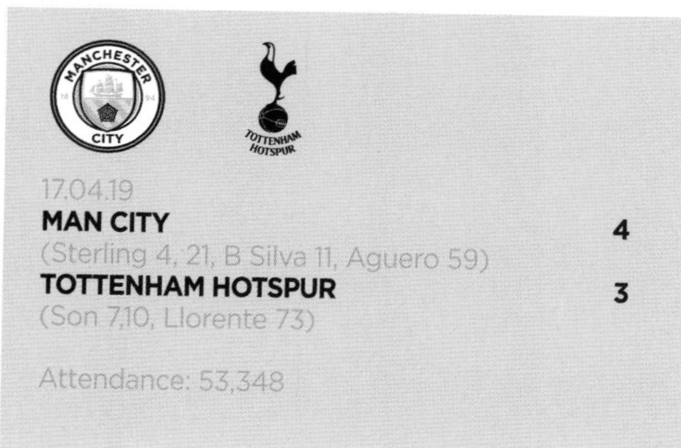

17.04.19

MAN CITY 4
(Sterling 4, 21, B Silva 11, Aguero 59)
TOTTENHAM HOTSPUR 3
(Son 7,10, Llorente 73)

Attendance: 53,348

Pep's men ahead on aggregate for the first time in the tie, but there was still plenty more drama to come. Spurs sub Fernando Llorente made it 4-3 when the ball appeared to strike his arm on 73 minutes and despite a lengthy VAR check by the referee, the goal stood.

Then, deep into added time, Sterling swept home what looked to be a dramatic winner – only for VAR to again go against City and disallow the goal. One moment the City players, management and fans were going crazy, the next it was Tottenham doing the same. Spurs were through on away goals and City's Champions League adventure was over for this season.

2018/19 FA COMMUNITY SHIELD

City were determined to begin the new season with the first silverware on offer to keep the feel-good factor going after the epic 2017/18 Centurions campaign.

The opponents were the 2018 FA Cup winners Chelsea, now managed by Maurizio Sarri, also keen to set a benchmark for the new season. City, meanwhile, started with new summer signing Riyad Mahrez and teenager Phil Foden also had the chance to impress at a sun-drenched Wembley Stadium.

With more than 72,000 fans in attendance, the game began with City quickly on top. In fact, it took just 13 minutes for Sergio Aguero to open his account for the new campaign, with the Argentine's smart low finish his 200th for the Club in all competitions.

Both teams had players missing following duty at the World Cup and the Blues started without Kevin De Bruyne, Ederson, David Silva and Raheem Sterling, while Chelsea were without their talisman Eden Hazard.

With searing temperatures slowing the pace of the game down, players were allowed water breaks as the game continued and just before the hour-mark, Aguero doubled City's lead after running on to Bernardo's clever pass to effectively end the contest.

Chelsea had no response of any note and City won the game 2-0 to land the season's first silverware. It was also a statement of intent that, no matter which competition the Blues were in, the goal was to win and compete all the way.

It was just the beginning of an unforgettable campaign...

05.08.18
MAN CITY **2**
CHELSEA 0

GOALS:
Aguero 13, 58

Attendance: 72,724

SILVERWARE
DOUBLE FOR CITY
ETIHAD AIRWAYS
SSE WOMEN'S FA CUP FINAL
v WEST HAM UNITED
4th MAY 2019
WEMBLEY STADIUM

City completed an impressive cup double in yet another memorable campaign for Nick Cushing's side.

Though the Blues fell just short in the FA Women's Super League, finishing runners-up to Arsenal, City qualified for the Champions League for the fourth successive season and dominated the domestic trophies on offer, beginning with the Continental Cup.

In what would be a long route to the final, City began with a 0-0 draw against Birmingham and a 5-4 victory on penalties. Next up, Leicester were comfortably dispatched 4-0 before the Blues travelled to Bristol City, winning 3-0.

The competition continued with goals aplenty including a 6-0 thrashing of Sheffield United, 4-0 win over Aston Villa and the 7-1 demolition of Brighton. Chelsea proved stiffer opposition in the semi-final before the final at Sheffield United's Bramall Lane. In a tense affair with Arsenal, City triumphed 4-2 on penalties to secure the Continental Cup, with Karen Bardsley saving two spot-kicks.

Three months later, Cushing's side were again celebrating a major trophy.

The FA Women's Cup offered City the chance of a unique double, with the quest beginning with a pair of 3-0 victories over Watford and Tottenham Hotspur. Next up, the Blues dispatched Liverpool - again by a score of 3-0 - to progress to the semi-finals where familiar old foes Chelsea awaited.

City had to wait until the 93rd minute to break the deadlock when Demi Stokes' cross was turned in by Magdalena Eriksson for a dramatic own goal and winner for the Blues. City were at Wembley again and looking for a second FA Women's Cup success, following the historic triumph over Birmingham in 2017.

In front of a crowd of 43,234, City faced West Ham United. Despite a goalless first period, the Blues upped the ante after the break with goals from Keira Walsh, Georgia Stanway and Lauren Hemp completing a 3-0 victory and a sixth major trophy in just five years.

AND THE WINNER IS...

After City's epic 2018/19 campaign, the awards came thick and fast...

LMA BARCLAYS MANAGER OF THE SEASON
Pep Guardiola

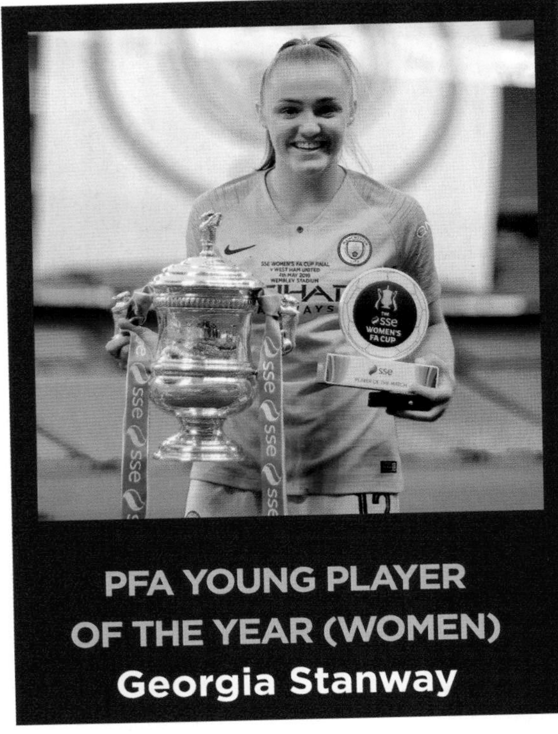

PFA YOUNG PLAYER OF THE YEAR (WOMEN)
Georgia Stanway

PFA YOUNG PLAYER OF THE YEAR
Raheem Sterling

PFA SPECIAL ACHIEVEMENT AWARD 2019
Steph Houghton

FOOTBALL WRITERS' ASSOCIATION PLAYER OF THE YEAR

Raheem Sterling

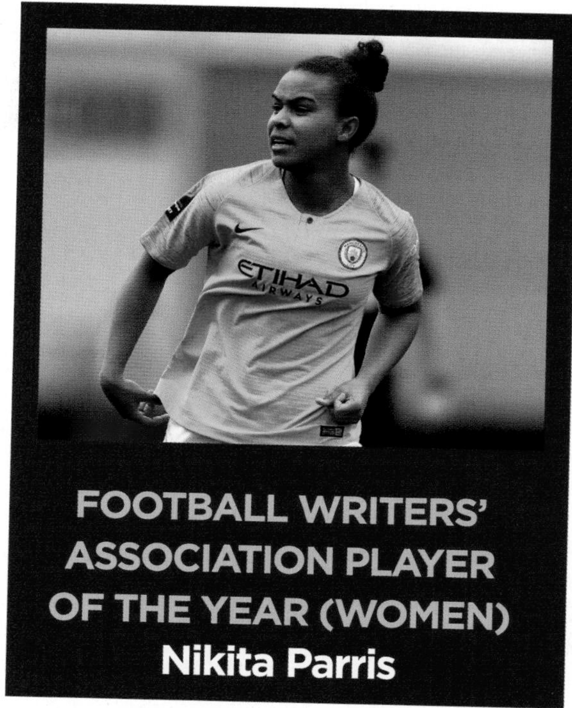

FOOTBALL WRITERS' ASSOCIATION PLAYER OF THE YEAR (WOMEN)

Nikita Parris

MANCHESTER CITY WOMEN PLAYER OF THE YEAR

Steph Houghton

MANCHESTER CITY WOMEN RISING STAR

Ellie Roebuck

PFA PREMIER LEAGUE TEAM OF THE YEAR

THE FA WOMEN'S SUPER LEAGUE TEAM OF THE YEAR

THANKS FOR EVERYTHING, CAPTAIN FANTASTIC

"HE DEFINES THE ESSENCE OF THE CLUB. FOR A DECADE HE HAS BEEN THE LIFEBLOOD, THE SOUL, AND BEATING HEART OF A SUPREMELY TALENTED SQUAD. A BOOMING VOICE IN THE DRESSING ROOM YET A QUIET AND MEASURED AMBASSADOR OFF IT, VINCENT CAN BE AS PROUD OF HIMSELF AS WE ARE OF HIM"

City Chairman, Khaldoon Al Mubarak